CUTTING EDGE CASES
IN THE LEGAL ENVIRONMENT OF BUSINESS

SECOND EDITION

CONSTANCE E. BAGLEY, J.D.
Graduate School of Business
Stanford University

RAKESH R. KHANNA, M.B.A., J.D.
Stanford University

WEST **West Educational Publishing Company**
an International Thomson Publishing company I T P®

Cincinnati • Albany • Boston • Detroit • Johannesburg • London • Madrid • Melbourne • Mexico City
New York • Pacific Grove • San Francisco • Scottsdale • Singapore • Tokyo • Toronto

Publisher/Team Director: Jack W. Calhoun
Acquisitions Editor: Scott D. Person
Development Editor: Jan Lamar
Production Editor: Peggy K. Buskey
Marketing Manager: Michael Worls

1 2 3 4 5 6 7 8 MA 5 4 3 2 1 0 9 8

Printed in the United States of America.

I(T)P®

International Thomson Publishing
West Educational Publishing is an ITP Company.
The ITP trademark is used under license.

CONTENTS

After a federal banking agency had made certain promises to induce solvent financial institutions to acquire failing savings and loans, Congress enacted a law that prevented the agency from fulfilling its promises. This case held that the acquiring financial institutions had a contractual right to recover from the government for its failure to fulfill its obligations.

PREFACE

CUTTING EDGE CASES (2nd ed.) fills the need for an up-to-the-minute collection of edited cases, using the court's own language, for courses in business law and the legal environment of business. This book is designed for several constituencies. On one level, it updates the often dramatic changes that have taken place in the law over the past three years. At the same time, it provides an opportunity for business students to explore cases in the court's own language in an expanded format. For other readers, the book provides a snapshot of judicial activity these past three years.

The cases presented were selected for timeliness, impact, coherence, and diversity. For example, *Reno v. American Civil Liberties Union* is the first U.S. Supreme Court case to consider what First Amendment protections extend to the Internet. The U.S. Supreme Court abandoned 30 years of antitrust precedent in *State Oil Company v. Kahn*, when it held that maximum resale price maintenance is not per se illegal and must be analyzed under the rule of reason. Although most of the decisions were handed down by the U.S. Supreme Court, several U.S. Court of Appeals opinions are also included.

A few of the cases selected may appear at first to have only a tenuous connection to the legal environment of business. However, each case demonstrates the current approach of the courts to key areas. For example, the U.S. Supreme Court case of *United States v. Lopez* addresses the constitutionality of federal legislation aimed at keeping guns away from school areas. The holding of the case illustrates the court's recent scrutiny of federal legislation based on the Constitution's Commerce Clause. Similarly, Justice Ginsburg's analysis in *United States v. Virginia* of the Virginia Military Institute's refusal to admit females suggests how gender-based discrimination may be analyzed in the work place. In short, cases dealing strictly with business law are not the only cases that affect the legal environment of business.

The past three years have witnessed a great deal of change in the law. With the appointment of Justices Ginsburg and Breyer to the U.S. Supreme Court, new alliances have formed on the Court and the political nature of the law has become much more apparent. The comments of Justice Scalia in *United States v. Virginia* and *Romer v. Evans* reveal the increasingly divided views of the Justices. This divisiveness will undeniably affect decisions for years to come.

The expanded treatment of the cases allows students to explore the nature of decisions more thoroughly, scrutinizing the reasoning and considering a competing argument presented by the dissent. Although it may be tempting to discount the importance of a dissenting opinion, one must remember that as a court's composition changes, the reasoning of today's dissent may carry tomorrow's majority.

The cases are presented as follows: Introductory history and facts of the case are summarized and presented in the **Background** section. The disposition of the case is then presented under the heading **Held**. Under **Opinion**, the cases are presented in the court's own language, edited only for space constraints. Almost all footnotes and citations have been omitted. Ellipses (three dots) are used to indicate that a portion of the court's language (other than citations and footnotes) has been omitted. An indented ellipsis indicates the omission of one or more paragraphs. Due to space constraints, concurrences and dissents are sometimes omitted.

ADARAND CONSTRUCTORS, INC. V. FEDERICO PENA

SUPREME COURT OF THE UNITED STATES

115 S. Ct. 2097

Decided June 12, 1995

"'[A] free people whose institutions are founded upon the doctrine of equality,' should tolerate no retreat from the principle that government may treat people differently because of their race only for the most compelling reasons."

Background: Adarand Constructors, Inc. (Adarand) submitted the lowest bid for the guardrail portion of a federal highway project, but the prime contractor selected a higher bid by a minority-owned firm. A federal program gave the prime contractor a financial incentive to hire a subcontractor certified as a small business controlled by socially and economically disadvantaged individuals, and required the prime contractor to presume that such individuals include certain minorities.

Adarand brought an action against Federico Pena, the Secretary of Transportation, challenging the constitutionality of the federal program on the grounds that its use of race-based presumptions violated the equal protection component of the Fifth Amendment's Due Process Clause. The Federal District Court granted summary judgment in favor of the defendant, Secretary Pena, upholding the federal program. Adarand appealed and the U.S. Court of Appeals affirmed. Adarand appealed.

Held: All racial classifications, whether imposed by federal, state, or local government, must be analyzed by the reviewing court under strict scrutiny. Because the Court of Appeals analyzed the case in terms of intermediate scrutiny, the Supreme Court remanded the case to the Court of Appeals so that the Court of Appeals could determine whether the challenged program satisfied strict scrutiny. [*Eds.*: In August 1997, the Court of Appeals held that the federal program failed to satisfy strict scrutiny and was therefore unconstitutional.]

Opinion: Justice O'CONNOR announced the judgment of the Court and delivered an opinion with respect to Parts I, II, III-A, III-B, III-D, and IV, which is for the Court except insofar as it might be inconsistent with the views expressed in Justice SCALIA's concurrence, and an opinion with respect to Part III-C in which Justice KENNEDY joins.

. . .

I

. . .

These fairly straightforward facts implicate a complex scheme of federal statutes and regulations, to which we now turn. The Small Business Act declares it to be "the policy of the United States that small business concerns, [and] small business concerns owned and controlled by socially and economically disadvantaged individuals, . . . shall have the maximum practicable opportunity to participate in the performance of contracts let by any Federal agency." The Act defines "socially disadvantaged individuals" as "those who have been subjected to racial or ethnic prejudice or cultural bias because of their identity as a member of a group without regard to their individual qualities," and it defines "economically disadvantaged individuals" as "those socially disadvantaged individuals whose ability to compete in the free enterprise system has been impaired due to diminished capital and credit opportunities as compared to others in the same business area who are not socially disadvantaged."

In furtherance of the policy stated . . . the Act establishes "[t]he Government-wide goal for participation by small business concerns owned and controlled by socially and economically disadvantaged individuals" at "not less than 5 percent of the total value of all prime contract and subcontract awards for each fiscal year." It also requires the head of each Federal agency to set agency-specific goals for participation by businesses controlled by socially and economically disadvantaged individuals.

The Small Business Administration (SBA) has implemented these statutory directives in a variety of ways, two of which are relevant here. One is the "8(a) program," which is available to small businesses controlled by socially and economically disadvantaged individuals as the SBA has defined those terms. The 8(a) program confers a wide range of benefits on participating businesses one of which is automatic eligibility for subcontractor compensation provisions of the kind at issue in this case. . . . To participate in the 8(a) program, a business must be "small," . . . and it must be 51% owned by individuals who qualify as "socially and economically disadvantaged." The SBA presumes that Black, Hispanic, Asian Pacific, Subcontinent Asian, and Native Americans, as well as "members of other groups designated from time to time by SBA," are "socially disadvantaged." It also allows any individual not a member of a listed group to prove social disadvantage "on the basis of clear and convincing evidence". . . . Social disadvantage is not enough to establish eligibility, however; SBA also requires each 8(a) program participant to prove "economic disadvantage". . . .

The other SBA program relevant to this case is the "8(d) subcontracting program," which unlike the 8(a) program is limited to eligibility for subcontracting provisions like the one at issue here. In determining eligibility, the SBA presumes social disadvantage based on membership in certain minority groups, just as in the 8(a) program, and again appears to require an individualized, although "less restrictive," showing of economic disadvantage. A different set of regulations, however, says that members of minority groups wishing to participate in the 8(d) subcontracting program are entitled to a race-based presumption of social and economic disadvantage. We are left with some uncertainty as to whether participation in the 8(d) subcontracting program requires an individualized showing of economic disadvantage. In any event, in both the 8(a) and the 8(d) programs, the presumptions of disadvantage are rebuttable if a third party comes forward with evidence suggesting that the participant is not, in fact, either economically or socially disadvantaged.

The contract giving rise to the dispute in this case came about as a result of the Surface Transportation and Uniform Relocation Assistance Act of 1987, a [Department of Transportation (DOT)] appropriations measure. Section 106(c)(1) of STURAA provides that "not less than 10 percent" of the appropriated funds "shall be expended with small business concerns owned and controlled by socially and economically disadvantaged individuals." STURAA adopts the Small Business Act's definition of "socially and economically disadvantaged individual," including the applicable race-based presumptions, and adds that "women shall be presumed to be socially and economically disadvantaged individuals for purposes of this subsection." STURAA also requires the Secretary of Transportation to establish "minimum uniform criteria for State governments to use in certifying whether a concern qualifies for purposes of this subsection". . . . Those regulations say that the certifying authority should presume both social and economic disadvantage (i.e., eligibility to participate) if the applicant belongs to certain racial groups, or is a woman. As with the SBA programs, third parties may come forward with evidence in an effort to rebut the presumption of disadvantage for a particular business. [The DOT established the Subcontracting Compensation Clause program, whereby prime contractors were given a financial incentive to hire subcontractors certified as small businesses controlled by socially and economically disadvantaged individuals.]

. . .

II

. . .

III

The Government urges that "[t]he Subcontracting Compensation Clause program is . . . a program based on disadvantage, not on race," and thus that it is subject only to "the most relaxed judicial scrutiny." To the extent that the statutes and regulations involved in this case are race neutral, we agree. The Government concedes, however, that "the race-based rebuttable presumption used in some certification determinations under the Subcontracting Compensation Clause" is subject to some heightened level of scrutiny. The parties disagree as to what that level should be. . . .

Adarand's claim arises under the Fifth Amendment to the Constitution, which provides that "No person shall . . . be deprived of life, liberty, or property, without due process of law." Although this Court has always understood that Clause to provide some measure of protection against arbitrary treatment by the Federal Government, it is not as explicit a guarantee of equal treatment as the Fourteenth Amendment, which provides that "No State shall . . . deny to any person within its jurisdiction the equal protection of the laws." Our cases have accorded varying degrees of significance to the difference in the language of those two Clauses. We think it necessary to revisit the issue here.

A

. . .

B

. . .

Despite lingering uncertainty in the details, however, the Court's cases through [*Richmond v. J.A. Croson Co.*][1] had established three general propositions with respect to governmental racial classifications. First, skepticism: "'[a]ny preference based on racial or ethnic criteria must necessarily receive a most searching examination.'" Second, consistency: "the standard of review under the Equal Protection Clause is not dependent on the race of those burdened or benefited by a particular classification," i.e., all racial classifications reviewable under the Equal Protection Clause must be strictly scrutinized. And third, congruence: "[e]qual protection analysis in the Fifth Amendment area is the same as that under the Fourteenth Amendment." Taken together, these three propositions lead to the conclusion that any person, of whatever race, has the right to demand that any governmental actor subject to the Constitution

---

[1] 488 U.S. 469 (1989).

justify any racial classification subjecting that person to unequal treatment under the strictest judicial scrutiny. . . .

. . . [T]he Court took a surprising turn. *Metro Broadcasting, Inc. v. FCC*[2] involved a Fifth Amendment challenge to two race-based policies of the Federal Communications Commission. In *Metro Broadcasting*, the Court repudiated the long-held notion that "it would be unthinkable that the same Constitution would impose a lesser duty on the Federal Government" than it does on a State to afford equal protection of the laws. It did so by holding that "benign" federal racial classifications need only satisfy intermediate scrutiny, even though *Croson* had recently concluded that such classifications enacted by a State must satisfy strict scrutiny. "[B]enign" federal racial classifications, the Court said, "—even if those measures are not 'remedial' in the sense of being designed to compensate victims of past governmental or societal discrimination— are constitutionally permissible to the extent that they serve important governmental objectives within the power of Congress and are substantially related to achievement of those objectives." The Court did not explain how to tell whether a racial classification should be deemed "benign," other than to express "confiden[ce] that an 'examination of the legislative scheme and its history' will separate benign measures from other types of racial classifications."

. . .

By adopting intermediate scrutiny as the standard of review for congressionally mandated "benign" racial classifications, *Metro Broadcasting* departed from prior cases in two significant respects. First, it turned its back on *Croson's* explanation of why strict scrutiny of all governmental racial classifications is essential. . . .

Second, *Metro Broadcasting* squarely rejected one of the three propositions established by the Court's earlier equal protection cases, namely, congruence between the standards applicable to federal and state racial classifications, and in so doing also undermined the other two—skepticism of all racial classifications, and consistency of treatment irrespective of the race of the burdened or benefited group. Under *Metro Broadcasting*, certain racial classifications ("benign" ones enacted by the Federal Government) should be treated less skeptically than others; and the race of the benefited group is critical to the determination of which standard of review to apply. *Metro Broadcasting* was thus a significant departure from much of what had come before it.

The three propositions undermined by *Metro Broadcasting* all derive from the basic principle that the Fifth and Fourteenth Amendments to the Constitution protect persons, not groups. It follows from that principle that all governmental action based on race—a group classification long recognized as "in most circumstances irrelevant and therefore prohibited,"—should be subjected to detailed judicial inquiry to ensure that the personal right to equal protection of the laws has not been infringed. These ideas have long been central to this Court's understanding of equal protection, and holding "benign" state and federal racial classifications to different standards does not square with them. "[A] free people whose institutions are founded upon the doctrine of equality," should tolerate no retreat from the principle that government may treat people differently because of their race only for the most compelling reasons. Accordingly, we hold today that all racial classifications, imposed by whatever federal, state, or local governmental actor, must be analyzed by a reviewing court under strict scrutiny. In other words, such classifications are constitutional only if they are narrowly tailored measures that further compelling governmental interests. To the extent that *Metro Broadcasting* is inconsistent with that holding, it is overruled.

---

[2] 497 U.S. 547 (1990).

. . .

C

"Although adherence to precedent is not rigidly required in constitutional cases, any departure from the doctrine of stare decisis demands special justification." In deciding whether this case presents such justification, we recall Justice Frankfurter's admonition that "stare decisis is a principle of policy and not a mechanical formula of adherence to the latest decision, however recent and questionable, when such adherence involves collision with a prior doctrine more embracing in its scope, intrinsically sounder, and verified by experience." Remaining true to an "intrinsically sounder" doctrine established in prior cases better serves the values of stare decisis than would following a more recently decided case inconsistent with the decisions that came before it; the latter course would simply compound the recent error and would likely make the unjustified break from previously established doctrine complete. In such a situation, "special justification" exists to depart from the recently decided case.

. . .

D

Our action today makes explicit what Justice Powell thought implicit . . . federal racial classifications, like those of a State, must serve a compelling governmental interest, and must be narrowly tailored to further that interest. . . .

. . .

Finally, we wish to dispel the notion that strict scrutiny is "strict in theory, but fatal in fact." The unhappy persistence of both the practice and the lingering effects of racial discrimination against minority groups in this country is an unfortunate reality, and government is not disqualified from acting in response to it. As recently as 1987, for example, every Justice of this Court agreed that the Alabama Department of Public Safety's "pervasive, systematic, and obstinate discriminatory conduct" justified a narrowly tailored race-based remedy. When race-based action is necessary to further a compelling interest, such action is within constitutional constraints if it satisfies the "narrow tailoring" test this Court has set out in previous cases.

IV

Because our decision today alters the playing field in some important respects, we think it best to remand the case to the lower courts for further consideration in light of the principles we have announced. . . . The Court of Appeals did not decide the question whether the interests served by the use of subcontractor compensation clauses are properly described as "compelling." It also did not address the question of narrow tailoring in terms of our strict scrutiny cases, by asking, for example, whether there was "any consideration of the use of race-neutral means to increase minority business participation" in government contracting or whether the program was appropriately limited such that it "will not last longer than the discriminatory effects it is designed to eliminate."

. . .

Accordingly, the judgment of the Court of Appeals is vacated, and the case is remanded for further proceedings consistent with this opinion.

It is so ordered.

Concurrence: Justice SCALIA, concurring in part and concurring in the judgment.

I join the opinion of the Court, except Part III-C, and except insofar as it may be inconsistent with the following: In my view, government can never have a "compelling interest" in discriminating on the basis of race in order to "make up" for past racial discrimination in the opposite direction. Individuals who have been wronged by unlawful racial discrimination should be made whole; but under our Constitution there can be no such thing as either a creditor or a debtor race. That concept is alien to the Constitution's focus upon the individual, and its rejection of dispositions based on race or based on blood. To pursue the concept of racial entitlement—even for the most admirable and benign of purposes—is to reinforce and preserve for future mischief the way of thinking that produced race slavery, race privilege and race hatred. In the eyes of government, we are just one race here. It is American.

It is unlikely, if not impossible, that the challenged program would survive under this understanding of strict scrutiny, but I am content to leave that to be decided on remand.

Concurrence: Justice THOMAS, concurring in part and concurring in the judgment.

I agree with the majority's conclusion that strict scrutiny applies to all government classifications based on race. I write separately, however, to express my disagreement with the premise underlying Justice STEVENS' and Justice GINSBURG's dissents: that there is a racial paternalism exception to the principle of equal protection. I believe that there is a "moral [and] constitutional equivalence," between laws designed to subjugate a race and those that distribute benefits on the basis of race in order to foster some current notion of equality. Government cannot make us equal; it can only recognize, respect, and protect us as equal before the law.

. . .

In my mind, government-sponsored racial discrimination based on benign prejudice is just as noxious as discrimination inspired by malicious prejudice. In each instance, it is racial discrimination, plain and simple.

Dissent: Justice STEVENS, dissenting.

Instead of deciding this case in accordance with controlling precedent, the Court today delivers a disconcerting lecture about the evils of governmental racial classifications. For its text the Court has selected three propositions, represented by the bywords "skepticism," "consistency," and "congruence." I shall comment on each of these propositions, then add a few words about stare decisis, and finally explain why I believe this Court has a duty to affirm the judgment of the Court of Appeals.

I

. . .

II

The Court's concept of "consistency" assumes that there is no significant difference between a decision by the majority to impose a special burden on the members of a minority race and a decision by the majority to provide a benefit to certain members of that minority notwithstanding its incidental burden on some members of the majority. In my opinion that assumption is untenable. . . .

. . .

III

The Court's concept of "congruence" assumes that there is no significant difference between a decision by the Congress of the United States to adopt an affirmative-action program and such a decision by a State or a municipality. In my opinion that assumption is untenable. It ignores important practical and legal differences between federal and state or local decisionmakers.

. . .

Ironically, after all of the time, effort, and paper this Court has expended in differentiating between federal and state affirmative action, the majority today virtually ignores the issue. It provides not a word of direct explanation for its sudden and enormous departure from the reasoning in past cases. Such silence, however, cannot erase the difference between Congress' institutional competence and constitutional authority to overcome historic racial subjugation and the States' lesser power to do so.

. . .

In my judgment, the Court's novel doctrine of "congruence" is seriously misguided. Congressional deliberations about a matter as important as affirmative action should be accorded far greater deference than those of a State or municipality.

IV

The Court's concept of stare decisis treats some of the language we have used in explaining our decisions as though it were more important than our actual holdings. In my opinion that treatment is incorrect.

This is the third time in the Court's entire history that it has considered the constitutionality of a federal affirmative-action program. On each of the two prior occasions . . . the Court upheld the program. . . .

. . .

. . . Providing a different answer to a similar question today cannot fairly be characterized as merely "restoring" previously settled law.

V

. . .

VI

My skeptical scrutiny of the Court's opinion leaves me in dissent. The majority's concept of "consistency" ignores a difference, fundamental to the idea of equal protection, between oppression and assistance. The majority's concept of "congruence" ignores a difference, fundamental to our constitutional system, between the Federal Government and the States. And the majority's concept of stare decisis ignores the force of binding precedent. I would affirm the judgment of the Court of Appeals.

Dissent: Justice GINSBURG, dissenting.

. . . I see no compelling cause for the intervention the Court has made in this case. I further agree with Justice STEVENS that, in this area, large deference is owed by the Judiciary to "Congress' institutional competence and constitutional authority to overcome historic racial subjugation." I write separately to underscore not the differences the several opinions in this case display, but the considerable field of agreement—the common understandings and concerns—revealed in opinions that together speak for a majority of the Court.

I

The statutes and regulations at issue, as the Court indicates, were adopted by the political branches in response to an "unfortunate reality": "[t]he unhappy persistence of both the practice and the lingering effects of racial discrimination against minority groups in this country." The United States suffers from those lingering effects because, for most of our Nation's history, the idea that "we are just one race," was not embraced. For generations, our lawmakers and judges were unprepared to say that there is in this land no superior race, no race inferior to any other. . . .

The divisions in this difficult case should not obscure the Court's recognition of the persistence of racial inequality and a majority's acknowledgment of Congress' authority to act affirmatively, not only to end discrimination, but also to counteract discrimination's lingering effects. . . .

Given this history and its practical consequences, Congress surely can conclude that a carefully designed affirmative action program may help to realize, finally, the "equal protection of the laws" the Fourteenth Amendment has promised since 1868.

II

The lead opinion uses one term, "strict scrutiny," to describe the standard of judicial review for all governmental classifications by race. But that opinion's elaboration strongly suggests that the strict standard announced is indeed "fatal" for classifications burdening groups that have suffered discrimination in our society. . . .

. . .

* * *

While I would not disturb the programs challenged in this case, and would leave their improvement to the political branches, I see today's decision as one that allows our precedent to evolve, still to be informed by and responsive to changing conditions.

BMW OF NORTH AMERICA, INC. V. IRA GORE, JR.

SUPREME COURT OF THE UNITED STATES

116 S. Ct. 1589

Decided May 20, 1996

"The fact that BMW is a large corporation rather than an impecunious individual does not diminish its entitlement to fair notice of the demands that the several States impose on the conduct of its business. Indeed, its status as an active participant in the national economy implicates the federal interest in preventing individual States from imposing undue burdens on interstate commerce."

Background: BMW of North America had a nationwide policy of not advising its dealers, and hence their customers, of predelivered damage to new cars when the cost of repair did not exceed three percent of the car's suggested retail price. As a result of this policy, Ira Gore, Jr. (Gore) unwittingly purchased a BMW that had been damaged in transit then repainted. When he learned that his BMW had been repainted, Gore brought an action against BMW, BMW's American distributor, and an authorized Alabama BMW dealer based on the distributor's failure to disclose that his BMW had been repainted after being damaged prior to delivery. An Alabama Circuit Court entered a judgment on a jury verdict awarding Gore compensatory damages of $4,000 and punitive damages of $4,000,000. The Alabama Supreme Court affirmed the judgment after reducing the punitive award to $2,000,000. BMW appealed.

Held: The award of $2,000,000 in punitive damages was grossly excessive in light of the low level of reprehensibility of conduct and the 500 to 1 ratio between the award and the actual harm to Gore. As a result, it violated the Due Process Clause of the Fourteenth Amendment of the U.S. Constitution.

Opinion: Justice STEVENS delivered the opinion of the Court.

The Due Process Clause of the Fourteenth Amendment prohibits a State from imposing a "'grossly excessive'" punishment on a tortfeasor. The wrongdoing involved in this case was the decision by a national distributor of automobiles not to advise its dealers, and hence their customers, of predelivery damage to new cars when the cost of repair amounted to less than 3 percent of the car's suggested retail price. The question presented is whether a $2 million punitive damages award to the purchaser of one of these cars exceeds the constitutional limit.

    I

    . . .

    II

Punitive damages may properly be imposed to further a State's legitimate interests in punishing unlawful conduct and deterring its repetition. In our federal system, States necessarily have considerable flexibility in determining the level of punitive damages that they will allow in different classes of cases and in any particular case.... Only when an award can fairly be categorized as "grossly excessive" in relation to these interests does it enter the zone of arbitrariness that violates the Due Process Clause of the Fourteenth Amendment. For that reason, the federal excessiveness inquiry appropriately begins with an identification of the state interests that a punitive award is designed to serve. We therefore focus our attention first on the scope of Alabama's legitimate interests in punishing BMW and deterring it from future misconduct.

No one doubts that a State may protect its citizens by prohibiting deceptive trade practices and by requiring automobile distributors to disclose presale repairs that affect the value of a new car. But the States need not, and in fact do not, provide such protection in a uniform manner. Some States rely on the judicial process to formulate and enforce an appropriate disclosure requirement by applying principles of contract and tort law. Other States have enacted various forms of legislation that define the disclosure obligations of automobile manufacturers, distributors, and dealers....

That diversity demonstrates that reasonable people may disagree about the value of a full disclosure requirement....

We may assume, arguendo, that it would be wise for every State to adopt Dr. Gore's preferred rule, requiring full disclosure of every presale repair to a car, no matter how trivial and regardless of its actual impact on the value of the car. But while we do not doubt that Congress has ample authority to enact such a policy for the entire Nation, it is clear that no single State could do so, or even impose its own policy choice on neighboring States....

We think it follows from these principles of state sovereignty and comity that a State may not impose economic sanctions on violators of its laws with the intent of changing the tortfeasors' lawful conduct in other States. Before this Court Dr. Gore argued that the large punitive damages award was necessary to induce BMW to change the nationwide policy that it adopted in 1983. But by attempting to alter BMW's nationwide policy, Alabama would be infringing on the policy choices of other States. To avoid such encroachment, the economic penalties that a State such as Alabama inflicts on those who transgress its laws, whether the penalties take the form of legislatively authorized fines or judicially imposed punitive damages, must be supported by the State's interest in protecting its own consumers and its own economy. Alabama may insist that BMW adhere to a particular disclosure policy in that State. Alabama does not have the power, however, to punish BMW for conduct that was lawful where it occurred and that had no impact on Alabama or its residents. Nor may Alabama impose sanctions on BMW in order to deter conduct that is lawful in other jurisdictions.

. . .

III

Elementary notions of fairness enshrined in our constitutional jurisprudence dictate that a person receive fair notice not only of the conduct that will subject him to punishment but also of the severity of the penalty that a State may impose. Three guideposts, each of which indicates that BMW did not receive adequate notice of the magnitude of the sanction that Alabama might impose for adhering to the nondisclosure policy adopted in 1983, lead us to the conclusion that the $2 million award against BMW is grossly excessive: the degree of reprehensibility of the nondisclosure; the disparity between the harm or potential harm suffered by Dr. Gore and his punitive damages award; and the difference between this remedy and the civil penalties authorized or imposed in comparable cases. We discuss these considerations in turn.

Degree of Reprehensibility

Perhaps the most important indicium of the reasonableness of a punitive damages award is the degree of reprehensibility of the defendant's conduct. As the Court stated nearly 150 years ago, exemplary damages imposed on a defendant should reflect "the enormity of his offense." This principle reflects the accepted view that some wrongs are more blameworthy than others. . . . In [*TXO Production Corp. v. Alliance Resources Corp.*][3], both the West Virginia Supreme Court and the Justices of this Court placed special emphasis on the principle that punitive damages may not be "grossly out of proportion to the severity of the offense". . . .

In this case, none of the aggravating factors associated with particularly reprehensible conduct is present. The harm BMW inflicted on Dr. Gore was purely economic in nature. . . . To be sure, infliction of economic injury, especially when done intentionally through affirmative acts of misconduct or when the target is financially vulnerable, can warrant a substantial penalty. But this observation does not convert all acts that cause economic harm into torts that are sufficiently reprehensible to justify a significant sanction in addition to compensatory damages.

. . .

That conduct is sufficiently reprehensible to give rise to tort liability, and even a modest award of exemplary damages, does not establish the high degree of culpability that warrants a substantial punitive damages award. Because this case exhibits none of the circumstances ordinarily associated with egregiously improper conduct, we are persuaded that BMW's conduct was not sufficiently reprehensible to warrant imposition of a $2 million exemplary damages award.

Ratio

The second and perhaps most commonly cited indicium of an unreasonable or excessive punitive damages award is its ratio to the actual harm inflicted on the plaintiff. The principle that exemplary damages must bear a "reasonable relationship" to compensatory damages has a long pedigree. . . .

In [*Pacific Mutual Life Ins. Co. v. Haslip*][4] we concluded that even though a punitive damages award of "more than 4 times the amount of compensatory damages," might be "close to the line," it did not "cross the line into the area of constitutional impropriety." *TXO*, following dicta in *Haslip*, refined this analysis by confirming that the proper inquiry is "'whether there is a reasonable relationship between the punitive damages award and the harm likely to result from the defendant's conduct as well as the harm that actually has occurred.'" Thus, in upholding the $10 million award in *TXO*, we relied on the difference between that figure and the harm to the victim that would have ensued if the tortious plan had succeeded. That difference suggested that the relevant ratio was not more than 10 to 1.

The $2 million in punitive damages awarded to Dr. Gore by the Alabama Supreme Court is 500 times the amount of his actual harm as determined by the jury. Moreover, there is no suggestion that Dr. Gore or any other BMW purchaser was threatened with any additional

[3] 509 U.S. 443 (1993).
[4] 499 U.S. 1 (1991).

potential harm by BMW's nondisclosure policy. The disparity in this case is thus dramatically greater than those considered in *Haslip* and *TXO*.

Of course, we have consistently rejected the notion that the constitutional line is marked by a simple mathematical formula, even one that compares actual and potential damages to the punitive award. . . . Once again, "we return to what we said . . . in *Haslip*: 'We need not, and indeed we cannot, draw a mathematical bright line between the constitutionally acceptable and the constitutionally unacceptable that would fit every case. We can say, however, that [a] general concer[n] of reasonableness . . . properly enter[s] into the constitutional calculus.'" In most cases, the ratio will be within a constitutionally acceptable range, and remittitur will not be justified on this basis. When the ratio is a breathtaking 500 to 1, however, the award must surely "raise a suspicious judicial eyebrow."

Sanctions for Comparable Misconduct

Comparing the punitive damages award and the civil or criminal penalties that could be imposed for comparable misconduct provides a third indicium of excessiveness. As Justice O'CONNOR has correctly observed, a reviewing court engaged in determining whether an award of punitive damages is excessive should "accord 'substantial deference' to legislative judgments concerning appropriate sanctions for the conduct at issue." In *Haslip*, the Court noted that although the exemplary award was "much in excess of the fine that could be imposed," imprisonment was also authorized in the criminal context. In this case the $2 million economic sanction imposed on BMW is substantially greater than the statutory fines available in Alabama and elsewhere for similar malfeasance.

The maximum civil penalty authorized by the Alabama Legislature for a violation of its Deceptive Trade Practices Act is $2,000; other States authorize more severe sanctions, with the maxima ranging from $5,000 to $10,000. . . . Moreover, at the time BMW's policy was first challenged, there does not appear to have been any judicial decision in Alabama or elsewhere indicating that application of that policy might give rise to such severe punishment.

The sanction imposed in this case cannot be justified on the ground that it was necessary to deter future misconduct without considering whether less drastic remedies could be expected to achieve that goal. The fact that a multimillion dollar penalty prompted a change in policy sheds no light on the question whether a lesser deterrent would have adequately protected the interests of Alabama consumers. . . .

IV

We assume, as the jur[y] in this case . . . found, that the undisclosed damage to the new BMWs affected their actual value. Notwithstanding the evidence adduced by BMW in an effort to prove that the repainted cars conformed to the same quality standards as its other cars, we also assume that it knew, or should have known, that as time passed the repainted cars would lose their attractive appearance more rapidly than other BMWs. Moreover, we of course accept the Alabama courts' view that the state interest in protecting its citizens from deceptive trade practices justifies a sanction in addition to the recovery of compensatory damages. We cannot, however, accept the conclusion of the Alabama Supreme Court that BMW's conduct was sufficiently egregious to justify a punitive sanction that is tantamount to a severe criminal penalty.

The fact that BMW is a large corporation rather than an impecunious individual does not diminish its entitlement to fair notice of the demands that the several States impose on the conduct of its business. Indeed, its status as an active participant in the national economy implicates the federal interest in preventing individual States from imposing undue burdens on interstate commerce. While each State has ample power to protect its own consumers, none may use the punitive damages deterrent as a means of imposing its regulatory policies on the entire Nation.

As in *Haslip*, we are not prepared to draw a bright line marking the limits of a constitutionally acceptable punitive damages award. Unlike that case, however, we are fully convinced that the grossly excessive award imposed in this case transcends the constitutional limit. . . .

The judgment is reversed, and the case is remanded for further proceedings not inconsistent with this opinion.

It is so ordered.

Dissent: Justice SCALIA, dissenting.

Today we see the latest manifestation of this Court's recent and increasingly insistent "concern about punitive damages that 'run wild.'" Since the Constitution does not make that concern any of our business, the Court's activities in this area are an unjustified incursion into the province of state governments.

In earlier cases that were the prelude to this decision, I set forth my view that a state trial procedure that commits the decision whether to impose punitive damages, and the amount, to the discretion of the jury, subject to some judicial review for "reasonableness," furnishes a defendant with all the process that is "due." I do not regard the Fourteenth Amendment's Due Process Clause as a secret repository of substantive guarantees against "unfairness"—neither the unfairness of an excessive civil compensatory award, nor the unfairness of an "unreasonable" punitive award. What the Fourteenth Amendment's procedural guarantee assures is an opportunity to contest the reasonableness of a damages judgment in state court; but there is no federal guarantee a damages award actually be reasonable.

. . .

I

. . .

At the time of adoption of the Fourteenth Amendment, it was well understood that punitive damages represent the assessment by the jury, as the voice of the community, of the measure of punishment the defendant deserved. Today's decision, though dressed up as a legal opinion, is really no more than a disagreement with the community's sense of indignation or outrage expressed in the punitive award of the Alabama jury, as reduced by the State Supreme Court. It reflects not merely, as the concurrence candidly acknowledges, "a judgment about a matter of degree," but a judgment about the appropriate degree of indignation or outrage, which is hardly an analytical determination.

There is no precedential warrant for giving our judgment priority over the judgment of state courts and juries on this matter. . . .

II

One might understand the Court's eagerness to enter this field, rather than leave it with the state legislatures, if it had something useful to say. In fact, however, its opinion provides virtually no guidance to legislatures, and to state and federal courts, as to what a "constitutionally proper" level of punitive damages might be.

. . .

III

In Part III of its opinion, the Court identifies "[t]hree guideposts" that lead it to the conclusion that the award in this case is excessive: degree of reprehensibility, ratio between punitive award and plaintiff's actual harm, and legislative sanctions provided for comparable misconduct. The legal significance of these "guideposts" is nowhere explored, but their necessary effect is to establish federal standards governing the hitherto exclusively state law of damages. Apparently (though it is by no means clear) all three federal "guideposts" can be overridden if "necessary to deter future misconduct,"—a loophole that will encourage state reviewing courts to uphold awards as necessary for the "adequat[e] protect[ion]" of state consumers. By effectively requiring state reviewing courts to concoct rationalizations—whether within the "guideposts" or through the loophole—to justify the intuitive punitive reactions of state juries, the Court accords neither category of institution the respect it deserves.

. . .

Dissent: Justice GINSBURG, dissenting.

The Court, I am convinced, unnecessarily and unwisely ventures into territory traditionally within the States' domain, and does so in the face of reform measures recently adopted or currently under consideration in legislative arenas. The Alabama Supreme Court, in this case, endeavored to follow this Court's prior instructions; and, more recently, Alabama's highest court has installed further controls on awards of punitive damages. I would therefore leave the state court's judgment undisturbed, and resist unnecessary intrusion into an area dominantly of state concern.

I

The respect due the Alabama Supreme Court requires that we strip from this case a false issue: no impermissible "extraterritoriality" infects the judgment before us; the excessiveness of the award is the sole issue genuinely presented. The Court ultimately so recognizes, but further clarification is in order. . . .

. . .

II

A

Alabama's Supreme Court reports that it "thoroughly and painstakingly" reviewed the jury's award, according to principles set out in its own pathmarking decisions and in this Court's opinions in *TXO* and *Pacific Mut. Life Ins. Co. v. Haslip*. The Alabama court said it gave weight to several factors, including BMW's deliberate ("reprehensible") presentation of refinished cars as new and undamaged, without disclosing that the value of those cars had been reduced by an estimated 10%, the financial position of the defendant, and the costs of litigation. These standards, we previously held, "impos[e] a sufficiently definite and meaningful constraint on the discretion of Alabama factfinders in awarding punitive damages." Alabama's highest court could have displayed its labor pains more visibly, but its judgment is nonetheless entitled to a presumption of legitimacy.

ANTONY BROWN V. PRO FOOTBALL, INC.

SUPREME COURT OF THE UNITED STATES

116 S. Ct. 2116

Decided June 20, 1996

"[I]t would be difficult, if not impossible, to require groups of employers and employees to bargain together, but at the same time to forbid them to make among themselves or with each other any of the competition-restricting agreements potentially necessary to make the process work or its results mutually acceptable."

Background: After their collective-bargaining agreement expired, the National Football League (NFL) and the NFL Players Association began to negotiate a new contract. The NFL presented a plan that would permit each of its teams to establish a "developmental squad" of substitute players, each of whom would be paid the same $1,000 weekly salary. The union disagreed, insisting that individual squad members should be free to negotiate their own salaries. When negotiations reached an impasse, the NFL unilaterally implemented the plan.

A number of squad players brought this antitrust suit, claiming that the agreement among the NFL teams to pay the players $1,000 per week restrained trade in violation of the Sherman Act. The Federal District Court entered a judgment for the players. The U.S. Court of Appeals reversed, holding that the NFL teams were immune from antitrust liability under the federal labor laws. The squad players appealed.

Held: The NFL teams were immune from antitrust liability because federal labor laws allow an agreement among several employers bargaining together to implement the terms of their last best good-faith wage offer after impasse.

Opinion: Justice BREYER delivered the opinion of the Court.

. . . This Court has previously found in the labor laws an implicit antitrust exemption that applies where needed to make the collective-bargaining process work. Like the Court of Appeals, we conclude that this need makes the exemption applicable in this case.

I

. . .

II

The immunity before us rests upon what this Court has called the "nonstatutory" labor exemption from the antitrust laws. The Court has implied this exemption from federal labor statutes, which set forth a national labor policy favoring free and private collective bargaining,

15

which require good-faith bargaining over wages, hours and working conditions, and which delegate related rulemaking and interpretive authority to the National Labor Relations Board.

   . . .

As a matter of logic, it would be difficult, if not impossible, to require groups of employers and employees to bargain together, but at the same time to forbid them to make among themselves or with each other any of the competition-restricting agreements potentially necessary to make the process work or its results mutually acceptable. Thus, the implicit exemption recognizes that, to give effect to federal labor laws and policies and to allow meaningful collective bargaining to take place, some restraints on competition imposed through the bargaining process must be shielded from antitrust sanctions.

The petitioners and their supporters concede, as they must, the legal existence of the exemption we have described. They also concede that, where its application is necessary to make the statutorily authorized collective-bargaining process work as Congress intended, the exemption must apply both to employers and to employees. . . . Consequently, the question before us is one of determining the exemption's scope: Does it apply to an agreement among several employers bargaining together to implement after impasse the terms of their last best good-faith wage offer? We assume that such conduct, as practiced in this case, is unobjectionable as a matter of labor law and policy. On that assumption, we conclude that the exemption applies.

Labor law itself regulates directly, and considerably, the kind of behavior here at issue— the postimpasse imposition of a proposed employment term concerning a mandatory subject of bargaining. Both the Board and the courts have held that, after impasse, labor law permits employers unilaterally to implement changes in preexisting conditions, but only insofar as the new terms meet carefully circumscribed conditions. For example, the new terms must be "reasonably comprehended" within the employer's preimpasse proposals (typically the last rejected proposals), lest by imposing more or less favorable terms, the employer unfairly undermined the union's status. The collective-bargaining proceeding itself must be free of any unfair labor practice, such as an employer's failure to have bargained in good faith. These regulations reflect the fact that impasse and an accompanying implementation of proposals constitute an integral part of the bargaining process.

Although the caselaw we have cited focuses upon bargaining by a single employer, no one here has argued that labor law does, or should, treat multiemployer bargaining differently in this respect. Indeed, Board and court decisions suggest that the joint implementation of proposed terms after impasse is a familiar practice in the context of multiemployer bargaining. . . .

Multiemployer bargaining itself is a well-established, important, pervasive method of collective bargaining, offering advantages to both management and labor. The upshot is that the practice at issue here plays a significant role in a collective-bargaining process that itself comprises an important part of the Nation's industrial relations system.

   . . .

If the antitrust laws apply, what are employers to do once impasse is reached? If all impose terms similar to their last joint offer, they invite an antitrust action premised upon identical behavior (along with prior or accompanying conversations) as tending to show a common understanding or agreement. If any, or all, of them individually impose terms that differ significantly from that offer, they invite an unfair labor practice charge. Indeed, how can employers safely discuss their offers together even before a bargaining impasse occurs? A pre-impasse discussion about, say, the practical advantages or disadvantages of a particular proposal, invites a later antitrust claim that they agreed to limit the kinds of action each would later take should an impasse occur. The same is true of postimpasse discussions aimed at renewed negotiations with the union. Nor would adherence to the terms of an expired collective-bargaining agreement eliminate a potentially plausible antitrust claim charging that they had "conspired" or tacitly "agreed" to do so, particularly if maintaining the status quo were not in the immediate economic self-interest of some. All this is to say that to permit antitrust liability here threatens to introduce instability and uncertainty into the collective-bargaining process, for antitrust law often forbids or discourages the kinds of joint discussions and behavior that the collective-bargaining process invites or requires.

We do not see any obvious answer to this problem. We recognize, as the Government suggests, that, in principle, antitrust courts might themselves try to evaluate particular kinds of employer understandings, finding them "reasonable" (hence lawful) where justified by collective-bargaining necessity. But any such evaluation means a web of detailed rules spun by many different nonexpert antitrust judges and juries, not a set of labor rules enforced by a single expert administrative body, namely the Labor Board. The labor laws give the Board, not antitrust courts, primary responsibility for policing the collective-bargaining process. And one of their objectives was to take from antitrust courts the authority to determine, through application of the antitrust laws, what is socially or economically desirable collective-bargaining policy.

III

Both petitioners and their supporters advance several suggestions for drawing the exemption boundary line short of this case. We shall explain why we find them unsatisfactory.

A

. . .

B

The Solicitor General argues that the exemption should terminate at the point of impasse. After impasse, he says, "employers no longer have a duty under the labor laws to maintain the status quo," and "are free as a matter of labor law to negotiate individual arrangements on an interim basis with the union."

Employers, however, are not completely free at impasse to act independently. The multi-employer bargaining unit ordinarily remains intact; individual employers cannot withdraw. The duty to bargain survives; employers must stand ready to resume collective bargaining. And individual employers can negotiate individual interim agreements with the union only insofar as those agreements are consistent with "the duty to abide by the results of group bargaining." Regardless, the absence of a legal "duty" to act jointly is not determinative. This Court has implied antitrust immunities that extend beyond statutorily required joint action to joint action that a statute "expressly or impliedly allows or assumes must also be immune."

More importantly, the simple "impasse" line would not solve the basic problem we have described above. Labor law permits employers, after impasse, to engage in considerable joint behavior, including joint lockouts and replacement hiring. Indeed, as a general matter, labor law often limits employers to four options at impasse: (1) maintain the status quo, (2) implement their last offer, (3) lock out their workers (and either shut down or hire temporary replacements), or (4) negotiate separate interim agreements with the union. What is to happen if the parties cannot reach an interim agreement? The other alternatives are limited. Uniform employer conduct is likely. Uniformity—at least when accompanied by discussion of the matter—invites antitrust attack. And such attack would ask antitrust courts to decide the lawfulness of activities intimately related to the bargaining process.

The problem is aggravated by the fact that "impasse" is often temporary; it may differ from bargaining only in degree; it may be manipulated by the parties for bargaining purposes; and it may occur several times during the course of a single labor dispute, since the bargaining process is not over when the first impasse is reached. How are employers to discuss future bargaining positions during a temporary impasse? Consider, too, the adverse consequences that flow from failing to guess how an antitrust court would later draw the impasse line. Employers who erroneously concluded that impasse had not been reached would risk antitrust liability were they collectively to maintain the status quo, while employers who erroneously concluded that impasse had occurred would risk unfair labor practice charges for prematurely suspending multiemployer negotiations.

. . .

C

Petitioners and their supporters argue in the alternative for a rule that would exempt postimpasse agreement about bargaining "tactics," but not postimpasse agreement about substantive "terms," from the reach of antitrust. They recognize, however, that both the Board and the courts have said that employers can, and often do, employ the imposition of "terms" as a bargaining "tactic." This concession as to joint "tactical" implementation would turn the presence of an antitrust exemption upon a determination of the employers' primary purpose or motive. But to ask antitrust courts, insulated from the bargaining process, to investigate an employer group's subjective motive is to ask them to conduct an inquiry often more amorphous than those we have previously discussed. And, in our view, a labor/antitrust line drawn on such a basis would too often raise the same related (previously discussed) problems.

D

. . .

Petitioners also say that irrespective of how the labor exemption applies elsewhere to multiemployer collective bargaining, professional sports is "special." We can understand how professional sports may be special in terms of, say, interest, excitement, or concern. But we do not understand how they are special in respect to labor law's antitrust exemption. We concede that the clubs that make up a professional sports league are not completely independent economic competitors, as they depend upon a degree of cooperation for economic survival. In the present context, however, that circumstance makes the league more like a single bargaining employer, which analogy seems irrelevant to the legal issue before us.

We also concede that football players often have special individual talents, and, unlike many unionized workers, they often negotiate their pay individually with their employers. But this characteristic seems simply a feature, like so many others, that might give employees (or employers) more (or less) bargaining power, that might lead some (or all) of them to favor a particular kind of bargaining, or that might lead to certain demands at the bargaining table. . . . [I]t would be odd to fashion an antitrust exemption that gave additional advantages to professional football players (by virtue of their superior bargaining power) that transport workers, coal miners, or meat packers would not enjoy.

. . . Ultimately, we cannot find a satisfactory basis for distinguishing football players from other organized workers. We therefore conclude that all must abide by the same legal rules.

* * * * * *

For these reasons, we hold that the implicit ("nonstatutory") antitrust exemption applies to the employer conduct at issue here. That conduct took place during and immediately after a collective-bargaining negotiation. It grew out of, and was directly related to, the lawful operation of the bargaining process. It involved a matter that the parties were required to negotiate collectively. And it concerned only the parties to the collective-bargaining relationship. . . .

The judgment of the Court of Appeals is affirmed.

It is so ordered.

Dissent: Justice STEVENS, dissenting.

. . . The unique features of this case lead me to conclude that the Court has reached a decision that conflicts with the basic purpose of both the antitrust laws and the national labor policy expressed in a series of congressional enactments.

I

. . .

Consistent with basic labor law policies, I agree with the Court that the judicially crafted labor exemption must also cover some collective action that employers take in response to a collective bargaining agent's demands for higher wages. Immunizing such action from antitrust scrutiny may facilitate collective bargaining over labor demands. So, too, may immunizing concerted employer action designed to maintain the integrity of the multi-employer bargaining unit, such as lockouts that are imposed in response to "a union strike tactic which threatens the destruction of the employers' interest in bargaining on a group basis."

In my view, however, neither the policies underlying the two separate statutory schemes, nor the narrower focus on the purpose of the nonstatutory exemption, provides a justification for exempting from antitrust scrutiny collective action initiated by employers to depress wages below the level that would be produced in a free market. Nor do those policies support a rule that would allow employers to suppress wages by implementing noncompetitive agreements among themselves on matters that have not previously been the subject of either an agreement with labor or even a demand by labor for inclusion in the bargaining process. That, however, is what is at stake in this litigation.

II

In light of the accommodation that has been struck between antitrust and labor law policy, it would be most ironic to extend an exemption crafted to protect collective action by employees to protect employers acting jointly to deny employees the opportunity to negotiate their salaries individually in a competitive market. Perhaps aware of the irony, the Court chooses to analyze this case as though it represented a typical impasse in an unexceptional multiemployer bargaining process. In so doing, it glosses over three unique features of the case that are critical to the inquiry into whether the policies of the labor laws require extension of the nonstatutory labor exemption to this atypical case.

First, in this market, unlike any other area of labor law implicated in the cases cited by the Court, player salaries are individually negotiated. . . .

Second, respondents concede that the employers imposed the wage restraint to force owners to comply with league-wide rules that limit the number of players that may serve on a team, not to facilitate a stalled bargaining process, or to revisit any issue previously subjected to bargaining. . . .

Third, although the majority asserts that the "club owners had bargained with the players' union over a wage issue until they reached impasse" that hardly constitutes a complete description of what transpired. . . .

. . .

III

. . .

IV

Congress is free to act to exempt the anticompetitive employer conduct that we review today. In the absence of such action, I do not believe it is for us to stretch the limited exemption that we have fashioned to facilitate the express statutory exemption created for labor's benefit so that unions must strike in order to restore a prior practice of individually negotiating salaries. . . .

. . .

Accordingly, I respectfully dissent.

DOCTOR'S ASSOCIATES, INC. AND NICK LOMBARDI V. PAUL CASAROTTO

SUPREME COURT OF THE UNITED STATES

116 S. Ct. 1652

Decided May 20, 1996

"Courts may not . . . invalidate arbitration agreements under state laws applicable only to arbitration provisions. By enacting § 2 [of the Federal Arbitration Act], we have several times said, Congress precluded States from singling out arbitration provisions for suspect status, requiring instead that such provisions be placed 'upon the same footing as other contracts.'"

Background: Subway sandwich-shop franchisees signed a standard franchise agreement, which included on page nine and in ordinary type a provision requiring all disputes arising under the agreement to be settled by arbitration. Nonetheless, these franchisees brought an action in state court against their Subway franchisor, Doctors Associates, Inc. (DAI), and its Montana development agent. Because of the mandatory arbitration provision in the franchise agreement, the trial court stayed the litigation, that is, did not allow it to go forward. The Subway franchisees appealed. The Montana Supreme Court reversed the trial court on the grounds that the standard franchise agreement's mandatory arbitration clause was unenforceable under a Montana statute that required that a mandatory arbitration clause be typed in underlined capital letters on the first page of the contract. The U.S. Supreme Court vacated the Montana Supreme Court's decision and remanded the case to the Montana Supreme Court for reconsideration in light of the Federal Arbitration Act (FAA). On remand, the Montana Supreme Court reaffirmed its prior opinion based on a finding that the FAA did not preempt the Montana statute. The franchisor appealed.

Held: Because the Montana statute conditioned the arbitration clause's enforceability on compliance with special notice requirements applicable only to arbitration agreements and the FAA prevents states from enacting laws specifically pertaining to written arbitration provisions, the FAA preempted the relevant Montana statute. Thus, the mandatory arbitration clause in the franchise agreement is enforceable.

Opinion: Justice GINSBURG delivered the opinion of the Court.

. . .

The Federal Arbitration Act . . . declares written provisions for arbitration "valid, irrevocable, and enforceable, save upon such grounds as exist at law or in equity for the revocation of any contract." Montana law, however, declares an arbitration clause unenforceable unless "[n]otice that [the] contract is subject to arbitration" is "typed in underlined capital letters on the first page of the contract." The question here presented is whether Montana's law is compatible with the federal Act. We hold that Montana's first-page notice requirement, which governs not "any contract," but specifically and solely contracts "subject to arbitration," conflicts with the FAA and is therefore displaced by the federal measure.

I

. . .

"States may regulate contracts, including arbitration clauses, under general contract law principles and they may invalidate an arbitration clause 'upon such grounds as exist at law or in equity for the revocation of any contract.' What States may not do is decide that a contract is fair enough to enforce all its basic terms (price, service, credit), but not fair enough to enforce its arbitration clause. The [Federal Arbitration] Act makes any such state policy unlawful, for that kind of policy would place arbitration clauses on an unequal 'footing,' directly contrary to the Act's language and Congress's intent."

. . .

II

Section 2 of the FAA provides that written arbitration agreements "shall be valid, irrevocable, and enforceable, save upon such grounds as exist at law or in equity for the revocation of any contract". . . . Thus, generally applicable contract defenses, such as fraud, duress or unconscionability, may be applied to invalidate arbitration agreements without contravening § 2.

Courts may not, however, invalidate arbitration agreements under state laws applicable only to arbitration provisions. By enacting § 2, we have several times said, Congress precluded States from singling out arbitration provisions for suspect status, requiring instead that such provisions be placed "upon the same footing as other contracts." Montana's § 27-5-114(4) directly conflicts with § 2 of the FAA because the State's law conditions the enforceability of arbitration agreements on compliance with a special notice requirement not applicable to contracts generally. The FAA thus displaces the Montana statute with respect to arbitration agreements covered by the Act.

. . .

* * *

For the reasons stated, the judgment of the Supreme Court of Montana is reversed, and the case is remanded for further proceedings not inconsistent with this opinion.

It is so ordered.

44 LIQUORMART, INC. AND PEOPLES SUPER LIQUOR STORES, INC. V. STATE OF RHODE ISLAND AND RHODE ISLAND LIQUOR STORES ASSOCIATION

SUPREME COURT OF THE UNITED STATES

116 S. Ct. 1495

Decided May 13, 1996

"[B]ans that target truthful, nonmisleading commercial messages rarely protect consumers from such harms. Instead, such bans often serve only to obscure an 'underlying governmental policy' that could be implemented without regulating speech."

Background: Rhode Island enacted statutes that prohibited the advertising of liquor prices except in the place of sale. Two liquor retailers, 44 Liquormart, Inc. and Peoples Super Liquor Stores, Inc., challenged these statutes on the grounds that they violated their right to free speech under the First Amendment of the U.S. Constitution. The Federal District Court held that the challenged statutes were unconstitutional because they did not directly advance Rhode Island's asserted interest in the promotion of temperance and were more extensive than necessary to serve that interest. The U.S. Court of Appeals held that the Rhode Island statutes were constitutional: They advanced Rhode Island's interest in the promotion of temperance and the Twenty-first Amendment (which ended the federal constitutional prohibition on the sale of liquor but gave the States the right to regulate the sale of liquor) gave the advertising ban a presumption of validity. The two liquor retailers appealed.

Held: The Rhode Island statutes prohibiting the advertising of liquor prices except in the place of sale were unconstitutional. Rhode Island's advertising ban was an abridgment of speech protected by the First Amendment and was not shielded from constitutional scrutiny by the Twenty-first Amendment. The challenged Rhode Island statutes did not directly advance Rhode Island's asserted interest in the promotion of temperance and were more extensive than necessary to serve that interest.

Opinion: Justice STEVENS announced the judgment of the Court and delivered the opinion of the Court with respect to Parts I, II, VII, and VIII, an opinion with respect to Parts III and V, in which Justice KENNEDY, Justice SOUTER, and Justice GINSBURG join, an opinion with respect to Part VI, in which Justice KENNEDY, Justice THOMAS, and Justice GINSBURG join, and an opinion with respect to Part IV, in which Justice KENNEDY and Justice GINSBURG join.

. . .

I

In 1956, the Rhode Island Legislature enacted two separate prohibitions against advertising the retail price of alcoholic beverages. The first applies to vendors licensed in Rhode Island as well as to out-of-state manufacturers, wholesalers, and shippers. It prohibits them from "advertising in any manner whatsoever" the price of any alcoholic beverage offered for sale in the State; the only exception is for price tags or signs displayed with the merchandise within licensed premises and not visible from the street. The second statute applies to the Rhode Island news media. It contains a categorical prohibition against the publication or broadcast of any advertisements—even those referring to sales in other States—that "make reference to the price of any alcoholic beverages."

. . .

II

Petitioners 44 Liquormart, Inc. (44 Liquormart), and Peoples Super Liquor Stores, Inc. (Peoples), are licensed retailers of alcoholic beverages. Petitioner 44 Liquormart operates a store in Rhode Island and petitioner Peoples operates several stores in Massachusetts that are patronized by Rhode Island residents. Peoples uses alcohol price advertising extensively in Massachusetts, where such advertising is permitted, but Rhode Island newspapers and other media outlets have refused to accept such ads.

Complaints from competitors about an advertisement placed by 44 Liquormart in a Rhode Island newspaper in 1991 generated enforcement proceedings that in turn led to the initiation of this litigation. The advertisement did not state the price of any alcoholic beverages. Indeed, it noted that "State law prohibits advertising liquor prices." The ad did, however, state the low prices at which peanuts, potato chips, and Schweppes mixers were being offered, identify various brands of packaged liquor, and include the word "WOW" in large letters next to pictures of vodka and rum bottles. Based on the conclusion that the implied reference to bargain prices for liquor violated the statutory ban on price advertising, the Rhode Island Liquor Control Administrator assessed a $400 fine.

After paying the fine, 44 Liquormart, joined by Peoples, filed this action against the administrator in the Federal District Court seeking a declaratory judgment that the two statutes and the administrator's implementing regulations violate the First Amendment and other provisions of federal law. . . . The parties stipulated that the price advertising ban is vigorously enforced, that Rhode Island permits "all advertising of alcoholic beverages excepting references to price outside the licensed premises," and that petitioners' proposed ads do not concern an illegal activity and presumably would not be false or misleading. The parties disagreed, however, about the impact of the ban on the promotion of temperance in Rhode Island. On that question the District Court heard conflicting expert testimony and reviewed a number of studies.

. . .

III

. . .

. . . It was not until the 1970's . . . that this Court held that the First Amendment protected the dissemination of truthful and nonmisleading commercial messages about lawful products and services.

In *Bigelow v. Virginia*,[5] we held that it was error to assume that commercial speech was entitled to no First Amendment protection or that it was without value in the marketplace of ideas. The following Term in *Virginia Bd. of Pharmacy v. Virginia Citizens Consumer Council, Inc.*,[6] we expanded on our holding in *Bigelow* and held that the State's blanket ban on advertising the price of prescription drugs violated the First Amendment.

Virginia Pharmacy Bd. reflected the conclusion that the same interest that supports regulation of potentially misleading advertising, namely the public's interest in receiving accurate commercial information, also supports an interpretation of the First Amendment that provides constitutional protection for the dissemination of accurate and nonmisleading commercial messages. . . .

The opinion . . . explained that a State's paternalistic assumption that the public will use truthful, nonmisleading commercial information unwisely cannot justify a decision to suppress it. . . .

On the basis of these principles, our early cases uniformly struck down several broadly based bans on truthful, nonmisleading commercial speech, each of which served ends unrelated to consumer protection. . . .

At the same time, our early cases recognized that the State may regulate some types of commercial advertising more freely than other forms of protected speech. Specifically, we explained that the State may require commercial messages to "appear in such a form, or include such additional information, warnings, and disclaimers, as are necessary to prevent its being deceptive," and that it may restrict some forms of aggressive sales practices that have the potential to exert "undue influence" over consumers.

. . .

. . . [A]lthough the special nature of commercial speech may require less than strict review of its regulation, special concerns arise from "regulations that entirely suppress commercial speech in order to pursue a nonspeech-related policy." In those circumstances, "a ban on speech could screen from public view the underlying governmental policy." As a result, . . . "special care" should attend the review of such blanket bans, and . . . "in recent years this Court has not approved a blanket ban on commercial speech unless the speech itself was flawed in some way, either because it was deceptive or related to unlawful activity."

IV

. . .

When a State regulates commercial messages to protect consumers from misleading, deceptive, or aggressive sales practices, or requires the disclosure of beneficial consumer information, the purpose of its regulation is consistent with the reasons for according constitutional protection to commercial speech and therefore justifies less than strict review. However, when a State entirely prohibits the dissemination of truthful, nonmisleading commercial messages for reasons unrelated to the preservation of a fair bargaining process, there is far less reason to depart from the rigorous review that the First Amendment generally demands.

. . .

---

[5] 421 U.S. 809 (1975).
[6] 425 U.S. 748 (1976).

It is the State's interest in protecting consumers from "commercial harms" that provides "the typical reason why commercial speech can be subject to greater governmental regulation than noncommercial speech." Yet bans that target truthful, nonmisleading commercial messages rarely protect consumers from such harms. Instead, such bans often serve only to obscure an "underlying governmental policy" that could be implemented without regulating speech. In this way, these commercial speech bans not only hinder consumer choice, but also impede debate over central issues of public policy.

Precisely because bans against truthful, nonmisleading commercial speech rarely seek to protect consumers from either deception or overreaching, they usually rest solely on the offensive assumption that the public will respond "irrationally" to the truth. The First Amendment directs us to be especially skeptical of regulations that seek to keep people in the dark for what the government perceives to be their own good. That teaching applies equally to state attempts to deprive consumers of accurate information about their chosen products. . . .

V

In this case, there is no question that Rhode Island's price advertising ban constitutes a blanket prohibition against truthful, nonmisleading speech about a lawful product. There is also no question that the ban serves an end unrelated to consumer protection. Accordingly, we must review the price advertising ban with "special care," mindful that speech prohibitions of this type rarely survive constitutional review.

The State argues that the price advertising prohibition should nevertheless be upheld because it directly advances the State's substantial interest in promoting temperance, and because it is no more extensive than necessary. . . .

In evaluating the ban's effectiveness in advancing the State's interest, we note that a commercial speech regulation "may not be sustained if it provides only ineffective or remote support for the government's purpose." For that reason, the State bears the burden of showing not merely that its regulation will advance its interest, but also that it will do so "to a material degree". . . .

. . .

Although the record suggests that the price advertising ban may have some impact on the purchasing patterns of temperate drinkers of modest means, the State has presented no evidence to suggest that its speech prohibition will significantly reduce market-wide consumption. . . .

. . .

As is evident, any conclusion that elimination of the ban would significantly increase alcohol consumption would require us to engage in the sort of "speculation or conjecture" that is an unacceptable means of demonstrating that a restriction on commercial speech directly advances the State's asserted interest. Such speculation certainly does not suffice when the State takes aim at accurate commercial information for paternalistic ends.

The State also cannot satisfy the requirement that its restriction on speech be no more extensive than necessary. It is perfectly obvious that alternative forms of regulation that would not involve any restriction on speech would be more likely to achieve the State's goal of promoting temperance. As the State's own expert conceded, higher prices can be maintained either by direct regulation or by increased taxation. Per capita purchases could be limited as is the case with prescription drugs. Even educational campaigns focused on the problems of excessive, or even moderate, drinking might prove to be more effective.

As a result, even under the less than strict standard that generally applies in commercial speech cases, the State has failed to establish a "reasonable fit" between its abridgment of speech and its temperance goal. It necessarily follows that the price advertising ban cannot survive the more stringent constitutional review that [*Central Hudson Gas & Elec. Corp. v. Public Serv. Comm'n of N.Y.*][7] itself concluded was appropriate for the complete suppression of truthful, nonmisleading commercial speech.

VI

. . .

From 1919 until 1933, the Eighteenth Amendment to the Constitution totally prohibited "the manufacture, sale, or transportation of intoxicating liquors" in the United States and its territories. Section 1 of the Twenty-first Amendment repealed that prohibition, and § 2 delegated to the several States the power to prohibit commerce in, or the use of, alcoholic beverages. The States' regulatory power over this segment of commerce is therefore largely "unfettered by the Commerce Clause."

. . .

. . . [A]lthough the Twenty-first Amendment limits the effect of the dormant Commerce Clause on a State's regulatory power over the delivery or use of intoxicating beverages within its borders, "the Amendment does not license the States to ignore their obligations under other provisions of the Constitution." That general conclusion reflects our specific holdings that the Twenty-first Amendment does not in any way diminish the force of the Supremacy Clause or the Equal Protection Clause. We see no reason why the First Amendment should not also be included in that list. Accordingly, we now hold that the Twenty-first Amendment does not qualify the constitutional prohibition against laws abridging the freedom of speech embodied in the First Amendment. The Twenty-first Amendment, therefore, cannot save Rhode Island's ban on liquor price advertising.

. . .

VIII

Because Rhode Island has failed to carry its heavy burden of justifying its complete ban on price advertising, we conclude that R.I. Gen. Laws §§ 3-8-7 and 3-8-8.1, as well as Regulation 32 of the Rhode Island Liquor Control Administration, abridge speech in violation of the First Amendment as made applicable to the States by the Due Process Clause of the Fourteenth Amendment. The judgment of the Court of Appeals is therefore reversed.

It is so ordered.

. . .

Concurrence: Justice O'CONNOR, with whom the Chief Justice, Justice SOUTER, and Justice BREYER join, concurring in the judgment.

Rhode Island prohibits advertisement of the retail price of alcoholic beverages, except at the place of sale. The State's only asserted justification for this ban is that it promotes temperance by increasing the cost of alcoholic beverages. I agree with the Court that Rhode Island's price-advertising ban is invalid. I would resolve this case more narrowly, however, by applying

---

[7] 447 U.S. 557 (1980).

our established . . . test to determine whether this commercial-speech regulation survives First Amendment scrutiny.

Under that test, we first determine whether the speech at issue concerns lawful activity and is not misleading, and whether the asserted governmental interest is substantial. If both these conditions are met, we must decide whether the regulation "directly advances the governmental interest asserted, and whether it is not more extensive than is necessary to serve that interest."

. . .

As we have explained, in order for a speech restriction to pass muster under the final prong, there must be a fit between the legislature's goal and method, "a fit that is not necessarily perfect, but reasonable; that represents not necessarily the single best disposition but one whose scope is in proportion to the interest served". . . . The availability of less burdensome alternatives to reach the stated goal signals that the fit between the legislature's ends and the means chosen to accomplish those ends may be too imprecise to withstand First Amendment scrutiny. . . .

Rhode Island offers one, and only one, justification for its ban on price advertising. Rhode Island says that the ban is intended to keep alcohol prices high as a way to keep consumption low. By preventing sellers from informing customers of prices, the regulation prevents competition from driving prices down and requires consumers to spend more time to find the best price for alcohol. The higher cost of obtaining alcohol, Rhode Island argues, will lead to reduced consumption.

The fit between Rhode Island's method and this particular goal is not reasonable. If the target is simply higher prices generally to discourage consumption, the regulation imposes too great, and unnecessary, a prohibition on speech in order to achieve it. The State has other methods at its disposal—methods that would more directly accomplish this stated goal without intruding on sellers' ability to provide truthful, nonmisleading information to customers. Indeed, Rhode Island's own expert conceded that "'the objective of lowering consumption of alcohol by banning price advertising could be accomplished by establishing minimum prices and/or by increasing sales taxes on alcoholic beverages.'" A tax, for example, is not normally very difficult to administer and would have a far more certain and direct effect on prices, without any restriction on speech. The principal opinion suggests further alternatives, such as limiting per capita purchases or conducting an educational campaign about the dangers of alcohol consumption. The ready availability of such alternatives—at least some of which would far more effectively achieve Rhode Island's only professed goal, at comparatively small additional administrative cost—demonstrates that the fit between ends and means is not narrowly tailored. . . .

. . .

Because Rhode Island's regulation fails even the less stringent standard . . . nothing here requires adoption of a new analysis for the evaluation of commercial speech regulation. The principal opinion acknowledges that "even under the less than strict standard that generally applies in commercial speech cases, the State has failed to establish a reasonable fit between its abridgment of speech and its temperance goal". . . .

. . .

JOHN HUDSON ET AL. V. UNITED STATES

SUPREME COURT OF THE UNITED STATES

118 S. Ct. 488

Decided Dec. 10, 1997

"To hold that the mere presence of a deterrent purpose renders such sanctions 'criminal' for double jeopardy purposes would severely undermine the Government's ability to engage in effective regulation of institutions. . . ."

Background: During the early and mid-1980s, John Hudson was the chairman and controlling shareholder of the First National Bank of Tipton and the First National Bank of Hammon. Tipton and Hammon are two very small towns in western Oklahoma.

The Office of the Comptroller of the Currency (OCC) investigated the Tipton and Hammon banks. The OCC found that Hudson had used his bank positions to arrange a series of loans that, while nominally made to third parties, were in reality made to Hudson in order to enable him to redeem bank stock that he had pledged as collateral on defaulted loans.

The OCC alleged that by causing the banks to make these loans, Hudson and two other bank officers violated various federal banking statutes and regulations. The OCC also alleged that the illegal loans resulted in losses to the Tipton and Hammon banks of almost $900,000 and contributed to the failure of those banks. In February 1989, the OCC assessed a "Civil Money Penalty" of $100,000 against Hudson. Later that year, the OCC issued Hudson notice that it intended to bar him from further participation in the conduct of "any insured depository institution."

Hudson resolved the OCC proceedings against him in October 1989 by agreeing (1) to pay $16,500, and (2) not to participate in any manner in the affairs of any banking institution without the written authorization of the OCC and all other relevant regulatory agencies. The two other bank officers reached a resolution.

In August 1992, Hudson and two other bank officers were indicted in the Western District of Oklahoma in a 22-count indictment on charges of criminal conspiracy and misapplication of bank funds. The violations charged in the indictment rested on the same lending transactions that formed the basis for the prior administrative actions brought by the OCC.

Hudson and his co-defendants moved to dismiss the indictment on double jeopardy grounds, but the Federal District Court denied the motions. The U.S. Court of Appeals affirmed. That court held, following *Halper*, that the actual fines imposed by the Government were not so grossly disproportional to the proven damages to the Government as to render the sanctions "punishment" for double jeopardy purposes. Hudson and his co-defendants appealed.

Held: The monetary penalties and occupational debarment imposed by the OCC were not so punitive in form and effect as to render them criminal for double jeopardy purposes. Because the Double Jeopardy Clause protects only against the imposition of multiple criminal punishments for the same offense, the Supreme Court affirmed the Tenth Circuit's decision.

Opinion: Chief Justice REHNQUIST delivered the opinion of the Court.

. . .

An examination . . . led the Office of the Comptroller of the Currency (OCC) to conclude that petitioners had used their bank positions to arrange a series of loans to third parties, in violation of various federal banking statutes and regulations. . . .

. . .

In October 1989, petitioners resolved the OCC proceedings against them by each entering into a "Stipulation and Consent Order." These consent orders provided that Hudson, Baresel, and Rackley would pay assessments of $16,500, $15,000, and $12,500 respectively. In addition, each petitioner agreed not to "participate in any manner" in the affairs of any banking institution without the written authorization of the OCC and all other relevant regulatory agencies.

In August 1992, petitioners were indicted . . . on charges of conspiracy, 18 U.S.C. § 371, misapplication of bank funds, §§ 656 and 2, and making false bank entries, § 1005.

The violations charged in the indictment rested on the same lending transactions that formed the basis for the prior administrative actions brought by OCC. . . .

. . .

The Double Jeopardy Clause provides that no "person [shall] be subject for the same offence to be twice put in jeopardy of life or limb." We have long recognized that the Double Jeopardy Clause does not prohibit the imposition of any additional sanction that could, "'in common parlance,'" be described as punishment. The Clause protects only against the imposition of multiple criminal punishments for the same offense.

Whether a particular punishment is criminal or civil is, at least initially, a matter of statutory construction. A court must first ask whether the legislature, "in establishing the penalizing mechanism, indicated either expressly or impliedly a preference for one label or the other." Even in those cases where the legislature "has indicated an intention to establish a civil penalty, we have inquired further whether the statutory scheme was so punitive either in purpose or effect," as to "transfor[m] what was clearly intended as a civil remedy into a criminal penalty."

In making this latter determination, the factors listed in *Kennedy v. Mendoza-Martinez*[8] provide useful guideposts, including (1) "[w]hether the sanction involves an affirmative disability or restraint"; (2) "whether it has historically been regarded as a punishment"; (3) "whether it comes into play only on a finding of scienter"; (4) "whether its operation will promote the traditional aims of punishment—retribution and deterrence"; (5) "whether the behavior to which it applies is already a crime"; (6) "whether an alternative purpose to which it may rationally be connected is assignable for it"; and (7) "whether it appears excessive in relation to the alternative purpose assigned."

---

[8] 372 U.S. 144 (1963).

It is important to note, however, that "these factors must be considered in relation to the statute on its face," and "only the clearest proof" will suffice to override legislative intent and transform what has been denominated a civil remedy into a criminal penalty.

. . .

Applying traditional double jeopardy principles to the facts of this case, it is clear that the criminal prosecution of these petitioners would not violate the Double Jeopardy Clause. It is evident that Congress intended the OCC money penalties and debarment sanctions imposed for violations of 12 U.S.C. §§ 84 and 375b to be civil in nature. As for the money penalties, both 12 U.S.C. §§ 93(b)(1) and 504(a), which authorize the imposition of monetary penalties for violations of §§ 84 and 375b respectively, expressly provide that such penalties are "civil." While the provision authorizing debarment contains no language explicitly denominating the sanction as civil, we think it significant that the authority to issue debarment orders is conferred upon the "appropriate Federal banking agenc[ies]." That such authority was conferred upon administrative agencies is . . . evidence that Congress intended to provide for a civil sanction.

Turning to the second stage of the . . . test, we find that there is little evidence, much less the clearest proof that we require, suggesting that either OCC money penalties or debarment sanctions are "so punitive in form and effect as to render them criminal despite Congress' intent to the contrary." First, neither money penalties nor debarment have historically been viewed as punishment. We have long recognized that "revocation of a privilege voluntarily granted," such as a debarment, "is characteristically free of the punitive criminal element." Similarly, "the payment of fixed or variable sums of money [is a] sanction which ha[s] been recognized as enforceable by civil proceedings since the original revenue law of 1789."

Second, the sanctions imposed do not involve an "affirmative disability or restraint," as that term is normally understood. While petitioners have been prohibited from further participating in the banking industry, this is "certainly nothing approaching the 'infamous punishment' of imprisonment." Third, neither sanction comes into play "only" on a finding of scienter. The provisions under which the money penalties were imposed, 12 U.S.C. §§ 93(b) and 504, allow for the assessment of a penalty against any person "who violates" any of the underlying banking statutes, without regard to the violator's state of mind. "Good faith" is considered by OCC in determining the amount of the penalty to be imposed, § 93(b)(2), but a penalty can be imposed even in the absence of bad faith. The fact that petitioners'"good faith" was considered in determining the amount of the penalty to be imposed in this case is irrelevant, as we look only to "the statute on its face" to determine whether a penalty is criminal in nature. Similarly, while debarment may be imposed for a "willful" disregard "for the safety or soundness of [an] insured depository institution," willfulness is not a prerequisite to debarment; it is sufficient that the disregard for the safety and soundness of the institution was "continuing."

Fourth, the conduct for which OCC sanctions are imposed may also be criminal (and in this case formed the basis for petitioners' indictments). This fact is insufficient to render the money penalties and debarment sanctions criminally punitive, particularly in the double jeopardy context.

Finally, we recognize that the imposition of both money penalties and debarment sanctions will deter others from emulating petitioners' conduct, a traditional goal of criminal punishment. But the mere presence of this purpose is insufficient to render a sanction criminal, as deterrence "may serve civil as well as criminal goals." For example, the sanctions at issue here, while intended to deter future wrongdoing, also serve to promote the stability of the banking industry. To hold that the mere presence of a deterrent purpose renders such sanctions "criminal" for double jeopardy purposes would severely undermine the Government's ability to engage in effective regulation of institutions such as banks.

In sum, there simply is very little showing, to say nothing of the "clearest proof" . . . that OCC money penalties and debarment sanctions are criminal. The Double Jeopardy Clause is therefore no obstacle to their trial on the pending indictments, and it may proceed. . . .

        . . .

JOSEPH ONCALE V. SUNDOWNER OFFSHORE SERVICES, INCORPORATED

SUPREME COURT OF THE UNITED STATES

118 S. Ct. 998

Decided March 4, 1998

"But statutory prohibitions often go beyond the principal evil to cover reasonably comparable evils, and it is ultimately the provisions of our laws rather than the principal concerns of our legislators by which we are governed."

Background: Joseph Oncale was employed by Sundowner Offshore Services as one of eight men on an oil platform in the Gulf of Mexico. On numerous occasions, Oncale was subjected to sex-related humiliation. Two of his supervisors worked in tandem to restrain Oncale as the other placed his penis on Oncale's neck on one occasion and on his arm on another. While on the company premises, one supervisor restrained Oncale as he showered, as the other forced a bar of soap into Oncale's anus, and both threatened anal rape. Both Oncale and his supervisors claimed to be heterosexual.

Oncale's complaints were unheeded by the company's Safety Compliance Clerk, who participated in the mistreatment. Oncale eventually resigned as a result of the continuing abuse, then filed a complaint for same-sex harassment under Title VII. The Federal District Court dismissed the claim, holding that Oncale, a male, had no cause of action under Title VII for harassment by male co-workers. The U.S. Court of Appeals affirmed. Oncale appealed.

Held: Sex discrimination consisting of same-sex sexual harassment is actionable under Title VII. There is no justification in Title VII's language or the Court's precedents for a categorical rule barring a claim of discrimination "because of . . . sex" merely because the plaintiff and the defendant are of the same sex. The Supreme Court remanded the case for further proceeding consistent with its opinion.

Opinion: Justice SCALIA delivered the opinion of the Court.

This case presents the question whether workplace harassment can violate Title VII's prohibition against "discriminat[ion] . . . because of . . . sex," when the harasser and the harassed employee are of the same sex.

I

The District Court having granted summary judgment for respondent, we must assume the facts to be as alleged by petitioner Joseph Oncale. The precise details are irrelevant to the legal point we must decide, and in the interest of both brevity and dignity we shall describe them only generally. In late October 1991, Oncale was working for respondent Sundowner Offshore Services on a Chevron U.S.A., Inc., oil platform in the Gulf of Mexico. He was employed as a roustabout on an eight-man crew which included respondents John Lyons, Danny Pippen, and Brandon Johnson. Lyons, the crane operator, and Pippen, the driller, had supervisory authority. . . . On several occasions, Oncale was forcibly subjected to sex related, humiliating actions against him by Lyons, Pippen and Johnson in the presence of the rest of the crew. Pippen and Lyons also physically assaulted Oncale in a sexual manner, and Lyons threatened him with rape.

Oncale's complaints to supervisory personnel produced no remedial action; in fact, the company's Safety Compliance Clerk, Valent Hohen, told Oncale that Lyons and Pippen "picked [on] him all the time too," and called him a name suggesting homosexuality. Oncale eventually quit—asking that his pink slip reflect that he "voluntarily left due to sexual harassment and verbal abuse." When asked at his deposition why he left Sundowner, Oncale stated "I felt that if I didn't leave my job, that I would be raped or forced to have sex."

. . .

II

Title VII of the Civil Rights Act of 1964 provides, in relevant part, that "[i]t shall be an unlawful employment practice for an employer . . . to discriminate against any individual with respect to his compensation, terms, conditions, or privileges of employment, because of such individual's race, color, religion, sex, or national origin." We have held that this not only covers "terms" and "conditions" in the narrow contractual sense, but "evinces a congressional intent to strike at the entire spectrum of disparate treatment of men and women in employment." "When the workplace is permeated with discriminatory intimidation, ridicule, and insult that is sufficiently severe or pervasive to alter the conditions of the victim's employment and create an abusive working environment, Title VII is violated."

Title VII's prohibition of discrimination "because of . . . sex" protects men as well as women, and in the related context of racial discrimination in the workplace we have rejected any conclusive presumption that an employer will not discriminate against members of his own race. "Because of the many facets of human motivation, it would be unwise to presume as a matter of law that human beings of one definable group will not discriminate against other members of that group." In *Johnson v. Transportation Agency, Santa Clara Cty.*,[9] a male employee claimed that his employer discriminated against him because of his sex when it preferred a female employee for promotion. Although we ultimately rejected the claim on other grounds, we did not consider it significant that the supervisor who made that decision was also a man. If our precedents leave any doubt on the question, we hold today that nothing in Title VII necessarily bars a claim of discrimination "because of . . . sex" merely because the plaintiff and the defendant (or the person charged with acting on behalf of the defendant) are of the same sex. Courts have had little trouble with that principle in cases like *Johnson*, where an employee claims to have been passed over for a job or promotion. But when the issue arises in the context of a "hostile environment" sexual harassment claim, the state and federal courts have taken a bewildering variety of stances. . . .

We see no justification in the statutory language or our precedents for a categorical rule excluding same-sex harassment claims from the coverage of Title VII. As some courts have observed, male-on-male sexual harassment in the workplace was assuredly not the principal evil

---

[9] 480 U.S. 616 (1987).

Congress was concerned with when it enacted Title VII. But statutory prohibitions often go beyond the principal evil to cover reasonably comparable evils, and it is ultimately the provisions of our laws rather than the principal concerns of our legislators by which we are governed. Title VII prohibits "discriminat[ion] . . . because of . . . sex" in the "terms" or "conditions" of employment. Our holding that this includes sexual harassment must extend to sexual harassment of any kind that meets the statutory requirements.

Respondents and their *amici* contend that recognizing liability for same-sex harassment will transform Title VII into a general civility code for the American workplace. But that risk is no greater for same-sex than for opposite sex harassment, and is adequately met by careful attention to the requirements of the statute. Title VII does not prohibit all verbal or physical harassment in the workplace; it is directed only at "discriminat[ion] . . . because of . . . sex." We have never held that workplace harassment, even harassment between men and women, is automatically discrimination because of sex merely because the words used have sexual content or connotations. "The critical issue, Title VII's text indicates, is whether members of one sex are exposed to disadvantageous terms or conditions of employment to which members of the other sex are not exposed."

Courts and juries have found the inference of discrimination easy to draw in most male-female sexual harassment situations, because the challenged conduct typically involves explicit or implicit proposals of sexual activity; it is reasonable to assume those proposals would not have been made to someone of the same sex. The same chain of inference would be available to a plaintiff alleging same-sex harassment, if there were credible evidence that the harasser was homosexual. But harassing conduct need not be motivated by sexual desire to support an inference of discrimination on the basis of sex. A trier of fact might reasonably find such discrimination, for example, if a female victim is harassed in such sex-specific and derogatory terms by another woman as to make it clear that the harasser is motivated by general hostility to the presence of women in the workplace. A same-sex harassment plaintiff may also, of course, offer direct comparative evidence about how the alleged harasser treated members of both sexes in a mixed-sex workplace. Whatever evidentiary route the plaintiff chooses to follow, he or she must always prove that the conduct at issue was not merely tinged with offensive sexual connotations, but actually constituted "discrimina[tion] . . . because of . . . sex."

And there is another requirement that prevents Title VII from expanding into a general civility code . . . the statute does not reach genuine but innocuous differences in the ways men and women routinely interact with members of the same sex and of the opposite sex. The prohibition of harassment on the basis of sex requires neither asexuality nor androgyny in the workplace; it forbids only behavior so objectively offensive as to alter the "conditions" of the victim's employment. "Conduct that is not severe or pervasive enough to create an objectively hostile or abusive work environment—an environment that a reasonable person would find hostile or abusive—is beyond Title VII's purview." We have always regarded that requirement as crucial, and as sufficient to ensure that courts and juries do not mistake ordinary socializing in the workplace—such as male-on-male horseplay or intersexual flirtation—for discriminatory "conditions of employment."

We have emphasized, moreover, that the objective severity of harassment should be judged from the perspective of a reasonable person in the plaintiff's position, considering "all the circumstances." In same-sex (as in all) harassment cases, that inquiry requires careful consideration of the social context in which particular behavior occurs and is experienced by its target. A professional football player's working environment is not severely or pervasively abusive, for example, if the coach smacks him on the buttocks as he heads onto the field—even if the same behavior would reasonably be experienced as abusive by the coach's secretary (male or female) back at the office. The real social impact of workplace behavior often depends on a constellation of surrounding circumstances, expectations, and relationships which are not fully captured by a simple recitation of the words used or the physical acts performed. Common sense, and an appropriate sensitivity to social context, will enable courts and juries to distinguish between simple teasing or roughhousing among members of the same sex, and conduct which a reasonable person in the plaintiff's position would find severely hostile or abusive.

III

Because we conclude that sex discrimination consisting of same-sex sexual harassment is actionable under Title VII, the judgment of the Court of Appeals for the Fifth Circuit is reversed, and the case is remanded for further proceedings consistent with this opinion.

It is so ordered.

PROCD, INCORPORATED V. MATTHEW ZEIDENBERG AND SILKEN MOUNTAIN WEB SERVICES, INC.

UNITED STATES COURT OF APPEALS FOR THE SEVENTH CIRCUIT

86 F.3d 1447

Decided June 20, 1996

"Much software is ordered over the Internet by purchasers who have never seen a box. Increasingly software arrives by wire. There is no box; there is only a stream of electrons, a collection of information that includes data, an application program, instructions, many limitations . . . and the terms of sale. . . . On Zeidenberg's arguments, these unboxed sales are unfettered by terms—so the seller has made a broad warranty and must pay consequential damages for any shortfalls in performance, two 'promises' that if taken seriously would drive prices through the ceiling or return transactions to the horse-and-buggy age."

Background: ProCD compiled information from more than 3,000 telephone directories into a single database. The database cost more than $10 million to compile and was expensive to keep current. ProCD sold a version of this database, called SelectPhone™, on CD-ROM disks. Each SelectPhone CD-ROM package contained within it a shrinkwrap license, i.e., a license that customers could not read when they made their decision to purchase SelectPhone but were deemed to have accepted when they opened the wrapping around the envelope containing the disks or clicked on the words "I accept" on the computer screen. Among other things, this shrinkwrap license prohibited the unauthorized resale of the SelectPhone database.

Matthew Zeidenberg purchased a SelectPhone package in Wisconsin. Zeidenberg indicated his agreement to the terms of the SelectPhone license by opening the packaging and by so indicating on the computer screen, but decided to ignore them. He formed Silken Mountain Web Services to resell the information in the SelectPhone database. Silken Mountain Web Services made the SelectPhone database available on the Internet to anyone willing to pay its price, which was less than that charged by ProCD. Zeidenberg purchased two additional SelectPhone packages, each with an updated version of the database, and made the latest information available via the Internet.

ProCD sued Zeidenberg and Silken Mountain Web Services, Inc. (Silken Mountain Web Services) for violating the license contained within the SelectPhone packages. The Federal District Court held in favor of Zeidenberg and Silken Mountain Web Services on the grounds: (1) the shrinkwrap license was not enforceable as a matter of state contract law, and (2) federal law preempted the enforcement of the license in question because it gave ProCD greater rights than those provided by federal copyright law. ProCD appealed.

Held: A shrinkwrap license whose terms are unknown at the time of purchase is still binding to the buyer unless its terms are objectionable on grounds applicable to contracts in general.

Federal copyright law does not preempt the enforcement of shrinkwrap licenses under state contract law.

Opinion: By EASTERBROOK, Circuit Judge.

. . .

I

. . .

II

. . . Zeidenberg . . . argue[s] . . . that placing the package of software on the shelf is an "offer," which the customer "accepts" by paying the asking price and leaving the store with the goods. In Wisconsin, as elsewhere, a contract includes only the terms on which the parties have agreed. One cannot agree to hidden terms, the judge concluded. So far, so good—but one of the terms to which Zeidenberg agreed by purchasing the software is that the transaction was subject to a license. Zeidenberg's position therefore must be that the printed terms on the outside of a box are the parties' contract—except for printed terms that refer to or incorporate other terms. But why would Wisconsin fetter the parties' choice in this way? Vendors can put the entire terms of a contract on the outside of a box only by using microscopic type, removing other information that buyers might find more useful (such as what the software does, and on which computers it works), or both. The "Read Me" file included with most software, describing system requirements and potential incompatibilities, may be equivalent to ten pages of type; warranties and license restrictions take still more space. Notice on the outside, terms on the inside, and a right to return the software for a refund if the terms are unacceptable (a right that the license expressly extends), may be a means of doing business valuable to buyers and sellers alike. Doubtless a state could forbid the use of standard contracts in the software business, but we do not think that Wisconsin has done so.

Transactions in which the exchange of money precedes the communication of detailed terms are common. Consider the purchase of insurance. The buyer goes to an agent, who explains the essentials (amount of coverage, number of years) and remits the premium to the home office, which sends back a policy. On the district judge's understanding, the terms of the policy are irrelevant because the insured paid before receiving them. Yet the device of payment, often with a "binder" (so that the insurance takes effect immediately even though the home office reserves the right to withdraw coverage later), in advance of the policy, serves buyers' interests by accelerating effectiveness and reducing transactions costs. Or consider the purchase of an airline ticket. The traveler calls the carrier or an agent, is quoted a price, reserves a seat, pays, and gets a ticket, in that order. The ticket contains elaborate terms, which the traveler can reject by canceling the reservation. To use the ticket is to accept the terms, even terms that in retrospect are disadvantageous. Just so with a ticket to a concert. The back of the ticket states that the patron promises not to record the concert; to attend is to agree. A theater that detects a violation will confiscate the tape and escort the violator to the exit. One could arrange things so that every concertgoer signs this promise before forking over the money, but that cumbersome way of doing things not only would lengthen queues and raise prices but also would scotch the sale of tickets by phone or electronic data service.

Consumer goods work the same way. Someone who wants to buy a radio set visits a store, pays, and walks out with a box. Inside the box is a leaflet containing some terms, the most important of which usually is the warranty, read for the first time in the comfort of home. By Zeidenberg's lights, the warranty in the box is irrelevant; every consumer gets the standard warranty implied by the UCC in the event the contract is silent; yet so far as we are aware no state disregards warranties furnished with consumer products. Drugs come with a list of ingredients on the outside and an elaborate package insert on the inside. The package insert describes drug interactions, contraindications, and other vital information—but, if Zeidenberg is right, the purchaser need not read the package insert, because it is not part of the contract.

Next consider the software industry itself. Only a minority of sales take place over the counter, where there are boxes to peruse. A customer may place an order by phone in response to a line item in a catalog or a review in a magazine. Much software is ordered over the Internet by purchasers who have never seen a box. Increasingly software arrives by wire. There is no box; there is only a stream of electrons, a collection of information that includes data, an application program, instructions, many limitations ("MegaPixel 3.14159 cannot be used with BytePusher 2.718"), and the terms of sale. The user purchases a serial number, which activates the software's features. On Zeidenberg's arguments, these unboxed sales are unfettered by terms—so the seller has made a broad warranty and must pay consequential damages for any shortfalls in performance, two "promises" that if taken seriously would drive prices through the ceiling or return transactions to the horse-and-buggy age.

According to the district court, the UCC does not countenance the sequence of money now, terms later. . . .

What then does the current version of the UCC have to say? We think that the place to start is § 2-204(1): "A contract for sale of goods may be made in any manner sufficient to show agreement, including conduct by both parties which recognizes the existence of such a contract." A vendor, as master of the offer, may invite acceptance by conduct, and may propose limitations on the kind of conduct that constitutes acceptance. A buyer may accept by performing the acts the vendor proposes to treat as acceptance. And that is what happened. ProCD proposed a contract that a buyer would accept by using the software after having an opportunity to read the license at leisure. This Zeidenberg did. He had no choice, because the software splashed the license on the screen and would not let him proceed without indicating acceptance. So although the district judge was right to say that a contract can be, and often is, formed simply by paying the price and walking out of the store, the UCC permits contracts to be formed in other ways. ProCD proposed such a different way, and without protest Zeidenberg agreed. Ours is not a case in which a consumer opens a package to find an insert saying "you owe us an extra $10,000" and the seller files suit to collect. Any buyer finding such a demand can prevent formation of the contract by returning the package, as can any consumer who concludes that the terms of the license make the software worth less than the purchase price. Nothing in the UCC requires a seller to maximize the buyer's net gains.

Section 2-606, which defines "acceptance of goods," reinforces this understanding. A buyer accepts goods under § 2-606(1)(b) when, after an opportunity to inspect, he fails to make an effective rejection under § 2-602(1). ProCD extended an opportunity to reject if a buyer should find the license terms unsatisfactory; Zeidenberg inspected the package, tried out the software, learned of the license, and did not reject the goods. We refer to § 2-606 only to show that the opportunity to return goods can be important; acceptance of an offer differs from acceptance of goods after delivery; but the UCC consistently permits the parties to structure their relations so that the buyer has a chance to make a final decision after a detailed review.

Some portions of the UCC impose additional requirements on the way parties agree on terms. A disclaimer of the implied warranty of merchantability must be "conspicuous" UCC § 2-316(2), incorporating UCC § 1-201(10). Promises to make firm offers, or to negate oral modifications, must be "separately signed." UCC §§ 2-205, 2-209(2). These special provisos reinforce the impression that, so far as the UCC is concerned, other terms may be as inconspicuous as the forum-selection clause on the back of the cruise ship ticket in [*Carnival Cruise Lines, Inc. v. Shute*].[10] Zeidenberg has not located any Wisconsin case—for that matter, any case in any state—holding that under the UCC the ordinary terms found in shrinkwrap licenses require any special prominence, or otherwise are to be undercut rather than enforced. In the end, the terms of the license are conceptually identical to the contents of the package. Just as no court would dream of saying that SelectPhone must contain 3,100 phone books rather than 3,000, or must have data no more than 30 days old, or must sell for $100 rather than $150— although any of these changes would be welcomed by the customer, if all other things were held constant—so, we believe, Wisconsin would not let the buyer pick and choose among terms. Terms of use are no less a part of "the product" than are the size of the database and the speed with which the software compiles listings. Competition among vendors, not judicial revision of a package's contents, is how consumers are protected in a market economy. ProCD has rivals, which may elect to compete by offering superior software, monthly updates, improved terms of use, lower price, or a better compromise among these elements. As we stressed above, adjusting terms in buyers' favor might help Matthew Zeidenberg today (he already has the software) but would lead to a response, such as a higher price, that might make consumers as a whole worse off.

III

The district court held that, even if Wisconsin treats shrinkwrap licenses as contracts, § 301(a) of the Copyright Act prevents their enforcement. The relevant part of § 301(a) preempts any "legal or equitable rights [under state law] that are equivalent to any of the exclusive rights within the general scope of copyright as specified by section 106 in works of authorship that are fixed in a tangible medium of expression and come within the subject matter of copyright as specified by sections 102 and 103." ProCD's software and data are "fixed in a tangible medium of expression," and the district judge held that they are "within the subject matter of copyright." The . . . judge thought that the data [was] . . . "within the subject matter of copyright". . . .

But are rights created by contract "equivalent to any of the exclusive rights within the general scope of copyright"? Three courts of appeals have answered "no." The district court disagreed with these decisions, but we think them sound. Rights "equivalent to any of the exclusive rights within the general scope of copyright" are rights established by law—rights that restrict the options of persons who are strangers to the author. Copyright law forbids duplication, public performance, and so on, unless the person wishing to copy or perform the work gets permission; silence means a ban on copying. A copyright is a right against the world. Contracts, by contrast, generally affect only their parties; strangers may do as they please, so contracts do not create "exclusive rights." Someone who found a copy of SelectPhone on the street would not be affected by the shrinkwrap license. . . .

. . . Think . . . about everyday transactions in intellectual property. A customer visits a video store and rents a copy of *Night of the Lepus*. The customer's contract with the store limits use of the tape to home viewing and requires its return in two days. May the customer keep the tape, on the ground that § 301(a) makes the promise unenforceable?

. . . Suppose ProCD hires a firm to scour the nation for telephone directories, promising to pay $100 for each that ProCD does not already have. The firm locates 100 new directories, which it sends to ProCD with an invoice for $10,000. ProCD incorporates the directories into its

---

[10] 499 U.S. 585 (1991).

database; does it have to pay the bill? Surely yes; *Aronson v. Quick Point Pencil Co.*[11] holds that promises to pay for intellectual property may be enforced even though federal law . . . offers no protection against third-party uses of that property. . . . Zeidenberg wants to use the data without paying the seller's price; if . . . Quick Point Pencil Co. could not do that, neither can Zeidenberg.

. . .

. . . Everyone remains free to copy and disseminate all 3,000 telephone books that have been incorporated into ProCD's database.[12] Anyone can add SIC codes and zip codes. ProCD's rivals have done so. Enforcement of the shrinkwrap license may even make information more readily available, by reducing the price ProCD charges to consumer buyers. To the extent licenses facilitate distribution of object code while concealing the source code (the point of a clause forbidding disassembly), they serve the same procompetitive functions as does the law of trade secrets. Licenses may have other benefits for consumers: many licenses permit users to make extra copies, to use the software on multiple computers, even to incorporate the software into the user's products. But whether a particular license is generous or restrictive, a simple two-party contract is not "equivalent to any of the exclusive rights within the general scope of copyright" and therefore may be enforced.

Reversed and remanded.

---

[11] 440 U.S. 257 (1979).

[12] *Eds.*: The U.S. Supreme Court held in *Feist Publications, Inc. v. Rural Telephone Service Co.*, 499 U.S. 340 (1991), that alphabetical listings of names, addresses, and phone numbers in the "white pages" are not protected under the federal Copyright Act.

JANET RENO V. AMERICAN CIVIL LIBERTIES UNION

SUPREME COURT OF THE UNITED STATES

117 S. Ct. 2329

Decided June 26, 1997

"As a matter of constitutional tradition, in the absence of evidence to the contrary, we presume that governmental regulation of the content of speech is more likely to interfere with the free exchange of ideas than to encourage it. The interest in encouraging freedom of expression in a democratic society outweighs any theoretical but unproven benefit of censorship."

Background: The American Civil Liberties Union (ACLU), which was joined by a variety of businesses, libraries, not-for-profit organizations, and educational societies, challenged the constitutionality of Sections 223(a) and 223(d) of the Communications Decency Act of 1996 (the CDA). Section 223(a) of the CDA criminalizes the interstate or international transmission of obscene or indecent communications by means of a telecommunications device. Section 223(d) of the CDA criminalizes the interstate or international transmission of any patently offensive communications to any person under the age of 18 through the use of an interactive computer service, such as an on-line service provider giving access to the Internet. The CDA provides two affirmative defenses. One covers those who take "good faith, reasonable, effective, and appropriate actions" to restrict access by minors to the prohibited communications. The other covers those who restrict access to covered material by requiring certain designated forms of age proof, such as a verified credit card or an adult identification number or code.

The Federal District Court issued a preliminary injunction against enforcement of Sections 223(a) and 223(d) of the CDA on the grounds that they violate the free speech protections afforded by the First Amendment and the due process protections afforded by the Fifth Amendment. Janet Reno, the U.S. Attorney General, appealed on behalf of the U.S. Government.

Held: The challenged sections of the CDA violate the First Amendment and are therefore unconstitutional, except for Section 223(a)'s ban on obscene speech which is constitutional because the First Amendment does not protect obscene speech.

Opinion: Justice STEVENS delivered the opinion of the Court.

At issue is the constitutionality of two statutory provisions enacted to protect minors from "indecent" and "patently offensive" communications on the Internet. Notwithstanding the legitimacy and importance of the congressional goal of protecting children from harmful materials, we agree with the three judge District Court that the statute abridges "the freedom of speech" protected by the First Amendment.

I

The District Court made extensive findings of fact, most of which were based on a detailed stipulation prepared by the parties. The findings describe the character and the dimensions of the Internet, the availability of sexually explicit material in that medium, and the problems confronting age verification for recipients of Internet communications. Because those findings provide the underpinnings for the legal issues, we begin with a summary of the undisputed facts.

The Internet

The Internet is an international network of interconnected computers. It is the outgrowth of what began in 1969 as a military program called "ARPANET," which was designed to enable computers operated by the military, defense contractors, and universities conducting defense related research to communicate with one another by redundant channels even if some portions of the network were damaged in a war. While the ARPANET no longer exists, it provided an example for the development of a number of civilian networks that, eventually linking with each other, now enable tens of millions of people to communicate with one another and to access vast amounts of information from around the world. The Internet is "a unique and wholly new medium of worldwide human communication."

The Internet has experienced "extraordinary growth." The number of "host" computers—those that store information and relay communications—increased from about 300 in 1981 to approximately 9,400,000 by the time of the trial in 1996. Roughly 60% of these hosts are located in the United States. About 40 million people used the Internet at the time of trial, a number that is expected to mushroom to 200 million by 1999.

Individuals can obtain access to the Internet from many different sources, generally hosts themselves or entities with a host affiliation. Most colleges and universities provide access for their students and faculty; many corporations provide their employees with access through an office network; many communities and local libraries provide free access; and an increasing number of storefront "computer coffee shops" provide access for a small hourly fee. Several major national "online services" such as America Online, CompuServe, the Microsoft Network, and Prodigy offer access to their own extensive proprietary networks as well as a link to the much larger resources of the Internet. These commercial online services had almost 12 million individual subscribers at the time of trial.

Anyone with access to the Internet may take advantage of a wide variety of communication and information retrieval methods. These methods are constantly evolving and difficult to categorize precisely. But, as presently constituted, those most relevant to this case are electronic mail ("e-mail"), automatic mailing list services ("mail exploders," sometimes referred to as "listservs"), "newsgroups," "chat rooms," and the "World Wide Web." All of these methods can be used to transmit text; most can transmit sound, pictures, and moving video images. Taken together, these tools constitute a unique medium—known to its users as "cyberspace"—located in no particular geographical location but available to anyone, anywhere in the world, with access to the Internet.

E-mail enables an individual to send an electronic message—generally akin to a note or letter—to another individual or to a group of addressees. The message is generally stored electronically, sometimes waiting for the recipient to check her "mailbox" and sometimes making its receipt known through some type of prompt. A mail exploder is a sort of e-mail group. Subscribers can send messages to a common e-mail address, which then forwards the message to the group's other subscribers. Newsgroups also serve groups of regular participants, but these postings may be read by others as well. There are thousands of such groups, each serving to foster an exchange of information or opinion on a particular topic running the gamut from, say, the music of Wagner to Balkan politics to AIDS prevention to the Chicago Bulls. About 100,000 new messages are posted every day. In most newsgroups, postings are automatically purged at regular intervals. In addition to posting a message that can be read later, two or more individuals wishing to communicate more immediately can enter a chat room to engage in real time dialogue—in other words, by typing messages to one another that appear almost immediately on the others' computer screens. The District Court found that at any given time "tens of thousands of users are engaging in conversations on a huge range of subjects." It is "no exaggeration to conclude that the content on the Internet is as diverse as human thought."

The best known category of communication over the Internet is the World Wide Web, which allows users to search for and retrieve information stored in remote computers, as well as, in some cases, to communicate back to designated sites. In concrete terms, the Web consists of a vast number of documents stored in different computers all over the world. Some of these documents are simply files containing information. However, more elaborate documents, commonly known as Web "pages," are also prevalent. Each has its own address—"rather like a telephone number." Web pages frequently contain information and sometimes allow the viewer to communicate with the page's (or "site's") author. They generally also contain "links" to other documents created by that site's author or to other (generally) related sites. Typically, the links are either blue or underlined text—sometimes images.

Navigating the Web is relatively straightforward. A user may either type the address of a known page or enter one or more keywords into a commercial "search engine" in an effort to locate sites on a subject of interest. A particular Web page may contain the information sought by the "surfer," or, through its links, it may be an avenue to other documents located anywhere on the Internet. Users generally explore a given Web page, or move to another, by clicking a computer "mouse" on one of the page's icons or links. Access to most Web pages is freely available, but some allow access only to those who have purchased the right from a commercial provider. The Web is thus comparable, from the readers' viewpoint, to both a vast library including millions of readily available and indexed publications and a sprawling mall offering goods and services.

From the publishers' point of view, it constitutes a vast platform from which to address and hear from a world wide audience of millions of readers, viewers, researchers, and buyers. Any person or organization with a computer connected to the Internet can "publish" information. Publishers include government agencies, educational institutions, commercial entities, advocacy groups, and individuals. Publishers may either make their material available to the entire pool of Internet users, or confine access to a selected group, such as those willing to pay for the privilege. "No single organization controls any membership in the Web, nor is there any centralized point from which individual Web sites or services can be blocked from the Web."

Sexually Explicit Material

Sexually explicit material on the Internet includes text, pictures, and chat and "extends from the modestly titillating to the hardest core." These files are created, named, and posted in the same manner as material that is not sexually explicit, and may be accessed either deliberately or unintentionally during the course of an imprecise search. "Once a provider posts its content on the Internet, it cannot prevent that content from entering any community." Thus, for example, "when the UCR/California Museum of Photography posts to its Web site nudes by Edward Weston and Robert Mapplethorpe to announce that its new exhibit will travel to Baltimore and New York City, those images are available not only in Los Angeles, Baltimore, and New York City, but also in Cincinnati, Mobile, or Beijing—wherever Internet users live. Similarly, the safer sex instructions that Critical Path posts to its Web site, written in street language so that the teenage receiver can understand them, are available not just in Philadelphia, but also in Provo and Prague."

Some of the communications over the Internet that originate in foreign countries are also sexually explicit.

Though such material is widely available, users seldom encounter such content accidentally. "A document's title or a description of the document will usually appear before the document itself . . . and in many cases the user will receive detailed information about a site's content before he or she need take the step to access the document. Almost all sexually explicit images are preceded by warnings as to the content." For that reason, the "odds are slim" that a user would enter a sexually explicit site by accident. Unlike communications received by radio or television, "the receipt of information on the Internet requires a series of affirmative steps more deliberate and directed than merely turning a dial. A child requires some sophistication and some ability to read to retrieve material and thereby to use the Internet unattended."

Systems have been developed to help parents control the material that may be available on a home computer with Internet access. . . .

Age Verification

The problem of age verification differs for different uses of the Internet. The District Court categorically determined that there "is no effective way to determine the identity or the age of a user who is accessing material through e-mail, mail exploders, newsgroups or chat rooms." The Government offered no evidence that there was a reliable way to screen recipients and participants in such fora for age. Moreover, even if it were technologically feasible to block minors' access to newsgroups and chat rooms containing discussions of art, politics or other subjects that potentially elicit "indecent" or "patently offensive" contributions, it would not be possible to block their access to that material and "still allow them access to the remaining content, even if the overwhelming majority of that content was not indecent."

Technology exists by which an operator of a Web site may condition access on the verification of requested information such as a credit card number or an adult password. Credit card verification is only feasible, however, either in connection with a commercial transaction in which the card is used, or by payment to a verification agency. Using credit card possession as a surrogate for proof of age would impose costs on non-commercial Web sites that would require many of them to shut down. For that reason, at the time of the trial, credit card verification was "effectively unavailable to a substantial number of Internet content providers." Moreover, the imposition of such a requirement "would completely bar adults who do not have a credit card and lack the resources to obtain one from accessing any blocked material."

Commercial pornographic sites that charge their users for access have assigned them passwords as a method of age verification. The record does not contain any evidence concerning the reliability of these technologies. Even if passwords are effective for commercial purveyors of indecent material, the District Court found that an adult password requirement would impose significant burdens on noncommercial sites, both because they would discourage users from accessing their sites and because the cost of creating and maintaining such screening systems would be "beyond their reach."

In sum, the District Court found:

> Even if credit card verification or adult password verification were implemented, the Government presented no testimony as to how such systems could ensure that the user of the password or credit card is in fact over 18. The burdens imposed by credit card verification and adult password verification systems make them effectively unavailable to a substantial number of Internet content providers.

II

. . .

III

. . .

The judgment of the District Court enjoins the Government from enforcing the prohibitions in § 223(a)(1)(B) insofar as they relate to "indecent" communications, but expressly preserves the Government's right to investigate and prosecute the obscenity or child pornography activities prohibited therein. The injunction against enforcement of §§ 223(d)(1) and (2) is unqualified because those provisions contain no separate reference to obscenity or child pornography.

The Government appealed under the Act's special review provisions. . . . In its appeal, the Government argues that the District Court erred in holding that the CDA violated both the First Amendment because it is overbroad and the Fifth Amendment because it is vague. While we discuss the vagueness of the CDA because of its relevance to the First Amendment overbreadth inquiry, we conclude that the judgment should be affirmed without reaching the Fifth Amendment issue. We begin our analysis by reviewing the principal authorities on which the Government relies. Then, after describing the overbreadth of the CDA, we consider the Government's specific contentions, including its submission that we save portions of the statute either by severance or by fashioning judicial limitations on the scope of its coverage.

IV

. . .

V

In *Southeastern Promotions, Ltd. v. Conrad*,[13] we observed that "[e]ach medium of expression . . . may present its own problems." Thus, some of our cases have recognized special justifications for regulation of the broadcast media that are not applicable to other speakers. In these cases, the Court relied on the history of extensive government regulation of the broadcast medium, the scarcity of available frequencies at its inception, and its "invasive" nature.

Those factors are not present in cyberspace. Neither before nor after the enactment of the CDA have the vast democratic fora of the Internet been subject to the type of government supervision and regulation that has attended the broadcast industry. Moreover, the Internet is not as "invasive" as radio or television. The District Court specifically found that "[c]ommunications over the Internet do not 'invade' an individual's home or appear on one's computer screen

---

[13] 420 U.S. 546 (1975).

unbidden. Users seldom encounter content 'by accident.'" It also found that "[a]lmost all sexually explicit images are preceded by warnings as to the content," and cited testimony that "'odds are slim' that a user would come across a sexually explicit sight by accident."

. . .

Finally, unlike the conditions that prevailed when Congress first authorized regulation of the broadcast spectrum, the Internet can hardly be considered a "scarce" expressive commodity. It provides relatively unlimited, low cost capacity for communication of all kinds. The Government estimates that "[a]s many as 40 million people use the Internet today, and that figure is expected to grow to 200 million by 1999." This dynamic, multifaceted category of communication includes not only traditional print and news services, but also audio, video, and still images, as well as interactive, real time dialogue. Through the use of chat rooms, any person with a phone line can become a town crier with a voice that resonates farther than it could from any soapbox. Through the use of Web pages, mail exploders, and newsgroups, the same individual can become a pamphleteer. As the District Court found, "the content on the Internet is as diverse as human thought." We agree with its conclusion that our cases provide no basis for qualifying the level of First Amendment scrutiny that should be applied to this medium.

VI

Regardless of whether the CDA is so vague that it violates the Fifth Amendment, the many ambiguities concerning the scope of its coverage render it problematic for purposes of the First Amendment. For instance, each of the two parts of the CDA uses a different linguistic form. The first uses the word "indecent," 47 U.S.C.A. § 223(a), while the second speaks of material that "in context, depicts or describes, in terms patently offensive as measured by contemporary community standards, sexual or excretory activities or organs," § 223(d). Given the absence of a definition of either term, this difference in language will provoke uncertainty among speakers about how the two standards relate to each other and just what they mean. Could a speaker confidently assume that a serious discussion about birth control practices, homosexuality, . . ., or the consequences of prison rape would not violate the CDA? This uncertainty undermines the likelihood that the CDA has been carefully tailored to the congressional goal of protecting minors from potentially harmful materials.

The vagueness of the CDA is a matter of special concern for two reasons. First, the CDA is a content based regulation of speech. The vagueness of such a regulation raises special First Amendment concerns because of its obvious chilling effect on free speech. Second, the CDA is a criminal statute. In addition to the opprobrium and stigma of a criminal conviction, the CDA threatens violators with penalties including up to two years in prison for each act of violation. The severity of criminal sanctions may well cause speakers to remain silent rather than communicate even arguably unlawful words, ideas, and images. . . .

. . .

In contrast to . . . our other previous cases, the CDA thus presents a greater threat of censoring speech that, in fact, falls outside the statute's scope. Given the vague contours of the coverage of the statute, it unquestionably silences some speakers whose messages would be entitled to constitutional protection. That danger provides further reason for insisting that the statute not be overly broad. The CDA's burden on protected speech cannot be justified if it could be avoided by a more carefully drafted statute.

VII

We are persuaded that the CDA lacks the precision that the First Amendment requires when a statute regulates the content of speech. In order to deny minors access to potentially harmful speech, the CDA effectively suppresses a large amount of speech that adults have a constitutional right to receive and to address to one another. That burden on adult speech is unacceptable if less restrictive alternatives would be at least as effective in achieving the legitimate purpose that the statute was enacted to serve.

In evaluating the free speech rights of adults, we have made it perfectly clear that "[s]exual expression which is indecent but not obscene is protected by the First Amendment". . . .

It is true that we have repeatedly recognized the governmental interest in protecting children from harmful materials. But that interest does not justify an unnecessarily broad suppression of speech addressed to adults. As we have explained, the Government may not "reduc[e] the adult population . . . to . . . only what is fit for children."

. . .

In arguing that the CDA does not so diminish adult communication, the Government relies on the incorrect factual premise that prohibiting a transmission whenever it is known that one of its recipients is a minor would not interfere with adult to adult communication. The findings of the District Court make clear that this premise is untenable. Given the size of the potential audience for most messages, in the absence of a viable age verification process, the sender must be charged with knowing that one or more minors will likely view it. Knowledge that, for instance, one or more members of a 100 person chat group will be minor—and therefore that it would be a crime to send the group an indecent message—would surely burden communication among adults.

The District Court found that at the time of trial existing technology did not include any effective method for a sender to prevent minors from obtaining access to its communications on the Internet without also denying access to adults. The Court found no effective way to determine the age of a user who is accessing material through e-mail, mail exploders, newsgroups, or chat rooms. As a practical matter, the Court also found that it would be prohibitively expensive for noncommercial—as well as some commercial—speakers who have Web sites to verify that their users are adults. These limitations must inevitably curtail a significant amount of adult communication on the Internet. By contrast, the District Court found that "[d]espite its limitations, currently available user based software suggests that a reasonably effective method by which parents can prevent their children from accessing sexually explicit and other material which parents may believe is inappropriate for their children will soon be widely available."

The breadth of the CDA's coverage is wholly unprecedented. Unlike the regulations upheld in *Ginsberg*[14] and *Pacifica*,[15] the scope of the CDA is not limited to commercial speech or commercial entities. Its open ended prohibitions embrace all nonprofit entities and individuals posting indecent messages or displaying them on their own computers in the presence of minors. The general, undefined terms "indecent" and "patently offensive" cover large amounts of non-pornographic material with serious educational or other value. Moreover, the "community standards" criterion as applied to the Internet means that any communication available to a nation wide audience will be judged by the standards of the community most likely to be offended by the message. The regulated subject matter includes any of the seven "dirty words" used in the *Pacifica* monologue, the use of which the Government's expert acknowledged could constitute a

---

[14] Ginsberg v. New York, 390 U.S. 629 (1968).
[15] FCC v. Pacifica Foundation, 438 U.S. 726 (1978).

felony. It may also extend to discussions about prison rape or safe sexual practices, artistic images that include nude subjects, and arguably the card catalogue of the Carnegie Library.

For the purposes of our decision, we need neither accept nor reject the Government's submission that the First Amendment does not forbid a blanket prohibition on all "indecent" and "patently offensive" messages communicated to a 17-year-old—no matter how much value the message may contain and regardless of parental approval. It is at least clear that the strength of the Government's interest in protecting minors is not equally strong throughout the coverage of this broad statute. Under the CDA, a parent allowing her 17-year-old to use the family computer to obtain information on the Internet that she, in her parental judgment, deems appropriate could face a lengthy prison term. Similarly, a parent who sent his 17-year-old college freshman information on birth control via e-mail could be incarcerated even though neither he, his child, nor anyone in their home community, found the material "indecent" or "patently offensive," if the college town's community thought otherwise.

The breadth of this content based restriction of speech imposes an especially heavy burden on the Government to explain why a less restrictive provision would not be as effective as the CDA. It has not done so. The arguments in this Court have referred to possible alternatives such as requiring that indecent material be "tagged" in a way that facilitates parental control of material coming into their homes, making exceptions for messages with artistic or educational value, providing some tolerance for parental choice, and regulating some portions of the Internet—such as commercial web sites—differently than others, such as chat rooms. Particularly in the light of the absence of any detailed findings by the Congress, or even hearings addressing the special problems of the CDA, we are persuaded that the CDA is not narrowly tailored if that requirement has any meaning at all.

VIII

In an attempt to curtail the CDA's facial overbreadth, the Government advances three additional arguments for sustaining the Act's affirmative prohibitions: (1) that the CDA is constitutional because it leaves open ample "alternative channels" of communication; (2) that the plain meaning of the Act's "knowledge" and "specific person" requirement significantly restricts its permissible applications; and (3) that the Act's prohibitions are "almost always" limited to material lacking redeeming social value.

The Government first contends that, even though the CDA effectively censors discourse on many of the Internet's modalities—such as chat groups, newsgroups, and mail exploders—it is nonetheless constitutional because it provides a "reasonable opportunity" for speakers to engage in the restricted speech on the World Wide Web. This argument is unpersuasive because the CDA regulates speech on the basis of its content. A "time, place, and manner" analysis is therefore inapplicable. It is thus immaterial whether such speech would be feasible on the Web (which, as the Government's own expert acknowledged, would cost up to $10,000 if the speaker's interests were not accommodated by an existing Web site, not including costs for database management and age verification). The Government's position is equivalent to arguing that a statute could ban leaflets on certain subjects as long as individuals are free to publish books. In invalidating a number of laws that banned leafletting on the streets regardless of their content—we explained that "one is not to have the exercise of his liberty of expression in appropriate places abridged on the plea that it may be exercised in some other place."

The Government also asserts that the "knowledge" requirement of both §§ 223(a) and (d), especially when coupled with the "specific child" element found in § 223(d), saves the CDA from overbreadth. Because both sections prohibit the dissemination of indecent messages only to persons known to be under 18, the Government argues, it does not require transmitters to "refrain from communicating indecent material to adults; they need only refrain from disseminating such materials to persons they know to be under 18."

This argument ignores the fact that most Internet fora—including chat rooms, news-groups, mail exploders, and the Web—are open to all comers. The Government's assertion that the knowledge requirement somehow protects the communications of adults is therefore untenable. Even the strongest reading of the "specific person" requirement of § 223(d) cannot save the statute. It would confer broad powers of censorship, in the form of a "heckler's veto," upon any opponent of indecent speech who might simply log on and inform the would be discoursers that his 17-year-old child—a "specific person . . . under 18 years of age," 47 U.S.C.A. § 223(d)(1)(A)—would be present.

Finally, we find no textual support for the Government's submission that material having scientific, educational, or other redeeming social value will necessarily fall outside the CDA's "patently offensive" and "indecent" prohibitions.

IX

The Government's three remaining arguments focus on the defenses provided in § 223(e)(5). First, relying on the "good faith, reasonable, effective, and appropriate actions" provision, the Government suggests that "tagging" provides a defense that saves the constitutionality of the Act. The suggestion assumes that transmitters may encode their indecent communications in a way that would indicate their contents, thus permitting recipients to block their reception with appropriate software. It is the requirement that the good faith action must be "effective" that makes this defense illusory. The Government recognizes that its proposed screening software does not currently exist. Even if it did, there is no way to know whether a potential recipient will actually block the encoded material. Without the impossible knowledge that every guardian in America is screening for the "tag," the transmitter could not reasonably rely on its action to be "effective."

For its second and third arguments concerning defenses—which we can consider together—the Government relies on the latter half of § 223(e)(5), which applies when the transmitter has restricted access by requiring use of a verified credit card or adult identification. Such verification is not only technologically available but actually is used by commercial providers of sexually explicit material. These providers, therefore, would be protected by the defense. Under the findings of the District Court, however, it is not economically feasible for most noncommercial speakers to employ such verification. Accordingly, this defense would not significantly narrow the statute's burden on noncommercial speech. Even with respect to the commercial pornographers that would be protected by the defense, the Government failed to adduce any evidence that these verification techniques actually preclude minors from posing as adults. Given that the risk of criminal sanctions "hovers over each content provider, like the proverbial sword of Damocles," the District Court correctly refused to rely on unproven future technology to save the statute. The Government thus failed to prove that the proffered defense would significantly reduce the heavy burden on adult speech produced by the prohibition on offensive displays.

We agree with the District Court's conclusion that the CDA places an unacceptably heavy burden on protected speech, and that the defenses do not constitute the sort of "narrow tailoring" that will save an otherwise patently invalid unconstitutional provision. . . .

X

At oral argument, the Government relied heavily on its ultimate fall back position: If this Court should conclude that the CDA is insufficiently tailored, it urged, we should save the statute's constitutionality by honoring the severability clause and construing nonseverable terms narrowly. In only one respect is this argument acceptable.

A severability clause requires textual provisions that can be severed. We will follow § 608's guidance by leaving constitutional textual elements of the statute intact in the one place where they are, in fact, severable. The "indecency" provision, 47 U.S.C.A. § 223(a), applies to "any comment, request, suggestion, proposal, image, or other communication which is obscene or indecent." Appellees do not challenge the application of the statute to obscene speech, which, they acknowledge, can be banned totally because it enjoys no First Amendment protection. As set forth by the statute, the restriction of "obscene" material enjoys a textual manifestation separate from that for "indecent" material, which we have held unconstitutional. Therefore, we will sever the term "or indecent" from the statute, leaving the rest of § 223(a) standing. In no other respect, however, can § 223(a) or § 223(d) be saved by such a textual surgery.

. . .

XI

. . .

For the foregoing reasons, the judgment of the district court is affirmed.

It is so ordered.

ROY ROMER v. RICHARD G. EVANS

SUPREME COURT OF THE UNITED STATES

116 S. Ct. 1620

Decided May 20, 1996

"It is not within our constitutional tradition to enact laws of this sort. Central both to the idea of the rule of law and to our own Constitution's guarantee of equal protection is the principle that government and each of its parts remain open on impartial terms to all who seek its assistance."

Background: After various Colorado municipalities passed ordinances banning discrimination based on sexual orientation in housing, employment, education, public accommodations, health and welfare services, and other transactions and activities, Colorado voters adopted by statewide referendum Amendment 2 to the Colorado State Constitution (Amendment 2). Amendment 2 precludes all legislative, executive, or judicial action at any level of state or local government designed to protect the status of persons based on their "homosexual, lesbian or bisexual orientation, conduct, practices or relationships."

Certain aggrieved homosexuals and municipalities commenced litigation in state court against certain Colorado state officials (including Colorado Governor Roy Romer) to declare Amendment 2 invalid and enjoin its enforcement. The trial court's grant of a preliminary injunction was sustained by the Colorado Supreme Court. The Colorado Supreme Court held that Amendment 2 was subject to strict scrutiny under the Equal Protection Clause of the Fourteenth Amendment because it infringed the fundamental right of gays and lesbians to participate in the political process. On remand, the trial court found that Amendment 2 failed to satisfy strict scrutiny. It enjoined Amendment 2's enforcement, and the Colorado Supreme Court affirmed. The Colorado state officials appealed.

Held: The status-based classification of persons in Amendment 2 violated the Equal Protection Clause.

Opinion: Justice KENNEDY delivered the opinion of the Court.

One century ago [in a dissent to the majority opinion in *Plessy v. Ferguson*, 163 U.S. 537 (1896), which upheld racial segregation on the theory of separate-but-equal], the first Justice Harlan admonished this Court that the Constitution "neither knows nor tolerates classes among citizens." Unheeded then, those words now are understood to state a commitment to the law's neutrality where the rights of persons are at stake. The Equal Protection Clause enforces this principle and today requires us to hold invalid a provision of Colorado's Constitution.

I

. . .

. . . [Amendment 2] reads:

"No Protected Status Based on Homosexual, Lesbian, or Bisexual Orientation. Neither the State of Colorado, through any of its branches or departments, nor any of its agencies, political subdivisions, municipalities or school districts, shall enact, adopt or enforce any statute, regulation, ordinance or policy whereby homosexual, lesbian or bisexual orientation, conduct, practices or relationships shall constitute or otherwise be the basis of or entitle any person or class of persons to have or claim any minority status, quota preferences, protected status or claim of discrimination. This Section of the Constitution shall be in all respects self-executing."

. . .

II

The State's principal argument in defense of Amendment 2 is that it puts gays and lesbians in the same position as all other persons. So, the State says, the measure does no more than deny homosexuals special rights. This reading of the amendment's language is implausible. We rely not upon our own interpretation of the amendment but upon the authoritative construction of Colorado's Supreme Court. The state court, deeming it unnecessary to determine the full extent of the amendment's reach, found it invalid even on a modest reading of its implications. The critical discussion of the amendment, set out in *Evans I*,[16] is as follows:

"The immediate objective of Amendment 2 is, at a minimum, to repeal existing statutes, regulations, ordinances, and policies of state and local entities that barred discrimination based on sexual orientation."

"The 'ultimate effect' of Amendment 2 is to prohibit any governmental entity from adopting similar, or more protective statutes, regulations, ordinances, or policies in the future unless the state constitution is first amended to permit such measures."

Sweeping and comprehensive is the change in legal status effected by this law. So much is evident from the ordinances that the Colorado Supreme Court declared would be void by operation of Amendment 2. Homosexuals, by state decree, are put in a solitary class with respect to transactions and relations in both the private and governmental spheres. The amendment withdraws from homosexuals, but no others, specific legal protection from the injuries caused by discrimination, and it forbids reinstatement of these laws and policies.

The change that Amendment 2 works in the legal status of gays and lesbians in the private sphere is far-reaching, both on its own terms and when considered in light of the structure and operation of modern anti-discrimination laws. That structure is well illustrated by contemporary statutes and ordinances prohibiting discrimination by providers of public accommodations. . . .

Colorado's state and municipal laws typify this emerging tradition of statutory protection and follow a consistent pattern. The laws first enumerate the persons or entities subject to a duty not to discriminate. The list goes well beyond the entities covered by the common law. The Boulder ordinance, for example, has a comprehensive definition of entities deemed places of

---

[16] Evans v. Romer, 854 P.2d 1270 (Colo. 1993).

"public accommodation." They include "any place of business engaged in any sales to the general public and any place that offers services, facilities, privileges, or advantages to the general public or that receives financial support through solicitation of the general public or through governmental subsidy of any kind." The Denver ordinance is of similar breadth, applying, for example, to hotels, restaurants, hospitals, dental clinics, theaters, banks, common carriers, travel and insurance agencies, and "shops and stores dealing with goods or services of any kind." These statutes and ordinances also depart from the common law by enumerating the groups or persons within their ambit of protection. Enumeration is the essential device used to make the duty not to discriminate concrete and to provide guidance for those who must comply. In following this approach, Colorado's state and local governments have not limited anti-discrimination laws to groups that have so far been given the protection of heightened equal protection scrutiny under our cases. Rather, they set forth an extensive catalogue of traits which cannot be the basis for discrimination, including age, military status, marital status, pregnancy, parenthood, custody of a minor child, political affiliation, physical or mental disability of an individual or of his or her associates—and, in recent times, sexual orientation.

Amendment 2 bars homosexuals from securing protection against the injuries that these public-accommodations laws address. That in itself is a severe consequence, but there is more. Amendment 2, in addition, nullifies specific legal protections for this targeted class in all transactions in housing, sale of real estate, insurance, health and welfare services, private education, and employment.

Not confined to the private sphere, Amendment 2 also operates to repeal and forbid all laws or policies providing specific protection for gays or lesbians from discrimination by every level of Colorado government. . . .

Amendment 2's reach may not be limited to specific laws passed for the benefit of gays and lesbians. It is a fair, if not necessary, inference from the broad language of the amendment that it deprives gays and lesbians even of the protection of general laws and policies that prohibit arbitrary discrimination in governmental and private settings. At some point in the systematic administration of these laws, an official must determine whether homosexuality is an arbitrary and thus forbidden basis for decision. Yet a decision to that effect would itself amount to a policy prohibiting discrimination on the basis of homosexuality, and so would appear to be no more valid under Amendment 2 than the specific prohibitions against discrimination the state court held invalid.

If this consequence follows from Amendment 2, as its broad language suggests, it would compound the constitutional difficulties the law creates. . . . In any event, even if, as we doubt, homosexuals could find some safe harbor in laws of general application, we cannot accept the view that Amendment 2's prohibition on specific legal protections does no more than deprive homosexuals of special rights. To the contrary, the amendment imposes a special disability upon those persons alone. Homosexuals are forbidden the safeguards that others enjoy or may seek without constraint. They can obtain specific protection against discrimination only by enlisting the citizenry of Colorado to amend the state constitution or perhaps, on the State's view, by trying to pass helpful laws of general applicability. This is so no matter how local or discrete the harm, no matter how public and widespread the injury. We find nothing special in the protections Amendment 2 withholds. These are protections taken for granted by most people either because they already have them or do not need them; these are protections against exclusion from an almost limitless number of transactions and endeavors that constitute ordinary civic life in a free society.

III

The Fourteenth Amendment's promise that no person shall be denied the equal protection of the laws must co-exist with the practical necessity that most legislation classifies for one purpose or another, with resulting disadvantage to various groups or persons. We have attempted to reconcile the principle with the reality by stating that, if a law neither burdens a fundamental right nor targets a suspect class, we will uphold the legislative classification so long as it bears a rational relation to some legitimate end.

Amendment 2 fails, indeed defies, even this conventional inquiry. First, the amendment has the peculiar property of imposing a broad and undifferentiated disability on a single named group, an exceptional and, as we shall explain, invalid form of legislation. Second, its sheer breadth is so discontinuous with the reasons offered for it that the amendment seems inexplicable by anything but animus toward the class that it affects; it lacks a rational relationship to legitimate state interests.

Taking the first point, even in the ordinary equal protection case calling for the most deferential of standards, we insist on knowing the relation between the classification adopted and the object to be attained. The search for the link between classification and objective gives substance to the Equal Protection Clause; it provides guidance and discipline for the legislature, which is entitled to know what sorts of laws it can pass; and it marks the limits of our own authority. In the ordinary case, a law will be sustained if it can be said to advance a legitimate government interest, even if the law seems unwise or works to the disadvantage of a particular group, or if the rationale for it seems tenuous. . . . By requiring that the classification bear a rational relationship to an independent and legitimate legislative end, we ensure that classifications are not drawn for the purpose of disadvantaging the group burdened by the law.

Amendment 2 confounds this normal process of judicial review. It is at once too narrow and too broad. It identifies persons by a single trait and then denies them protection across the board. The resulting disqualification of a class of persons from the right to seek specific protection from the law is unprecedented in our jurisprudence. The absence of precedent for Amendment 2 is itself instructive; "[d]iscriminations of an unusual character especially suggest careful consideration to determine whether they are obnoxious to the constitutional provision."

It is not within our constitutional tradition to enact laws of this sort. Central both to the idea of the rule of law and to our own Constitution's guarantee of equal protection is the principle that government and each of its parts remain open on impartial terms to all who seek its assistance. "'Equal protection of the laws is not achieved through indiscriminate imposition of inequalities.'" Respect for this principle explains why laws singling out a certain class of citizens for disfavored legal status or general hardships are rare. A law declaring that in general it shall be more difficult for one group of citizens than for all others to seek aid from the government is itself a denial of equal protection of the laws in the most literal sense. "The guaranty of 'equal protection of the laws is a pledge of the protection of equal laws.'"

. . .

A . . . related point is that laws of the kind now before us raise the inevitable inference that the disadvantage imposed is born of animosity toward the class of persons affected. "[I]f the constitutional conception of 'equal protection of the laws' means anything, it must at the very least mean that a bare . . . desire to harm a politically unpopular group cannot constitute a legitimate governmental interest." Even laws enacted for broad and ambitious purposes often can be explained by reference to legitimate public policies which justify the incidental disadvantages they impose on certain persons. Amendment 2, however, in making a general announcement that gays and lesbians shall not have any particular protections from the law, inflicts on them immediate, continuing, and real injuries that outrun and belie any legitimate justifications that may be claimed for it. We conclude that, in addition to the far-reaching deficiencies of Amendment 2 that we have noted, the principles it offends, in another sense, are conventional and venerable; a law must bear a rational relationship to a legitimate governmental purpose and Amendment 2 does not.

The primary rationale the State offers for Amendment 2 is respect for other citizens' freedom of association, and in particular the liberties of landlords or employers who have personal or religious objections to homosexuality. Colorado also cites its interest in conserving resources to fight discrimination against other groups. The breadth of the Amendment is so far removed from these particular justifications that we find it impossible to credit them. We cannot say that Amendment 2 is directed to any identifiable legitimate purpose or discrete objective. It is a status-based enactment divorced from any factual context from which we could discern a relationship to legitimate state interests; it is a classification of persons undertaken for its own sake, something the Equal Protection Clause does not permit. "[C]lass legislation . . . [is] obnoxious to the prohibitions of the Fourteenth Amendment. . . ."

We must conclude that Amendment 2 classifies homosexuals not to further a proper legislative end but to make them unequal to everyone else. This Colorado cannot do. A State cannot so deem a class of persons a stranger to its laws. Amendment 2 violates the Equal Protection Clause, and the judgment of the Supreme Court of Colorado is affirmed.

It is so ordered.

Dissent: Justice SCALIA, dissenting.

. . . The constitutional amendment before us here is not the manifestation of a "'bare . . . desire to harm'" homosexuals, but is rather a modest attempt by seemingly tolerant Coloradans to preserve traditional sexual mores against the efforts of a politically powerful minority to revise those mores through use of the laws. That objective, and the means chosen to achieve it, are not only unimpeachable under any constitutional doctrine hitherto pronounced (hence the opinion's heavy reliance upon principles of righteousness rather than judicial holdings); they have been specifically approved by the Congress of the United States and by this Court.

In holding that homosexuality cannot be singled out for disfavorable treatment, the Court contradicts a decision, unchallenged here, pronounced only 10 years ago, and places the prestige of this institution behind the proposition that opposition to homosexuality is as reprehensible as racial or religious bias. Whether it is or not is precisely the cultural debate that gave rise to the Colorado constitutional amendment (and to the preferential laws against which the amendment was directed). Since the Constitution of the United States says nothing about this subject, it is left to be resolved by normal democratic means, including the democratic adoption of provisions in state constitutions. This Court has no business imposing upon all Americans the resolution favored by the elite class from which the Members of this institution are selected, pronouncing that "animosity" toward homosexuality is evil. I vigorously dissent.

I

Let me first discuss Part II of the Court's opinion, its longest section, which is devoted to rejecting the State's arguments that Amendment 2 "puts gays and lesbians in the same position as all other persons," and "does no more than deny homosexuals special rights." The Court concludes that this reading of Amendment 2's language is "implausible" under the "authoritative construction" given Amendment 2 by the Supreme Court of Colorado.

. . .

. . . The amendment prohibits special treatment of homosexuals, and nothing more. It would not affect, for example, a requirement of state law that pensions be paid to all retiring state employees with a certain length of service; homosexual employees, as well as others, would be entitled to that benefit. But it would prevent the State or any municipality from making death-benefit payments to the "life partner" of a homosexual when it does not make such payments to the long-time roommate of a nonhomosexual employee. Or again, it does not affect the requirement of the State's general insurance laws that customers be afforded coverage without discrimination unrelated to anticipated risk. Thus, homosexuals could not be denied coverage, or charged a greater premium, with respect to auto collision insurance; but neither the State nor any municipality could require that distinctive health insurance risks associated with homosexuality (if there are any) be ignored.

. . .

II

I turn next to whether there was a legitimate rational basis for the substance of the constitutional amendment—for the prohibition of special protection for homosexuals. It is unsurprising that the Court avoids discussion of this question, since the answer is so obviously yes. The case most relevant to the issue before us today is not even mentioned in the Court's opinion: In *Bowers v. Hardwick*,[17] we held that the Constitution does not prohibit what virtually all States had done from the founding of the Republic until very recent years—making homosexual conduct a crime. . . . If it is constitutionally permissible for a State to make homosexual conduct criminal, surely it is constitutionally permissible for a State to enact other laws merely disfavoring homosexual conduct. . . .

. . .

III

The foregoing suffices to establish what the Court's failure to cite any case remotely in point would lead one to suspect: No principle set forth in the Constitution, nor even any imagined by this Court in the past 200 years, prohibits what Colorado has done here. But the case for Colorado is much stronger than that. What it has done is not only unprohibited, but eminently reasonable, with close, congressionally approved precedent in earlier constitutional practice.

. . .

IV

. . .

* * *

Today's opinion has no foundation in American constitutional law, and barely pretends to. The people of Colorado have adopted an entirely reasonable provision which does not even disfavor homosexuals in any substantive sense, but merely denies them preferential treatment. Amendment 2 is designed to prevent piecemeal deterioration of the sexual morality favored by a majority of Coloradans, and is not only an appropriate means to that legitimate end, but a means that Americans have employed before. Striking it down is an act, not of judicial judgment, but of political will. I dissent.

---

[17] 478 U.S. 186 (1986). [*Eds.*: *Bowers* upheld a state criminal conviction for sodomy.]

STATE OIL COMPANY V. BARKAT U. KHAN AND KHAN & ASSOCIATES, INC.

SUPREME COURT OF THE UNITED STATES

118 S. Ct. 275

Decided Nov. 4, 1997

"Our interpretation of the Sherman Act also incorporates the notion that condemnation of practices resulting in lower prices to consumers is 'especially costly' because 'cutting prices in order to increase business often is the very essence of competition.'"

Background: Barkat U. Khan and his corporation (Khan) entered into a contract with State Oil Company (State Oil) to lease and operate a gas station and convenience store owned by State Oil. The agreement provided that Khan would purchase the station's gasoline from State Oil at a price equal to a suggested retail price set by State Oil, less a margin of 3.25 cents per gallon. Under the agreement, Khan could charge any price to his customers, but if the price charged was higher than State Oil's suggested retail price, the excess was to be rebated to State Oil. Similarly, if Khan sold gasoline for less than the suggested retail price, it would reduce his 3.25 cent margin.

A year after Khan began operating the station, he fell behind in his lease payments to State Oil, which then notified Khan of its intent to terminate the agreement due to his breach and to evict him from the station. Khan then sued State Oil, alleging that it had engaged in price fixing in violation of the Sherman Act. The Federal District Court granted summary judgment for State Oil, holding that Khan did not allege a per se violation of the antitrust law and did not demonstrate antitrust injury or harm to competition. The U.S. Court of Appeals reversed, holding that the claim did allege a per se violation and that Khan could have suffered antitrust harm. State Oil appealed.

Held: A vertical maximum price contract, such as the Shell Oil contract, does not constitute a per se violation of the Sherman Antitrust Act. Prior precedent to the contrary is overruled. Because the Seventh Circuit analyzed the case based on overruled precedent, the Supreme Court vacated the Seventh Circuit judgment and remanded the case for further proceedings consistent with its opinion.

Opinion: Justice O'CONNOR delivered the opinion of the Court.

Under §1 of the Sherman Act "[e]very contract, combination . . . , or conspiracy, in restraint of trade" is illegal. In *Albrecht v. Herald Co.*,[18] this Court held that vertical maximum price fixing is a per se violation of that statute. In this case, we are asked to reconsider that decision in light of subsequent decisions of this Court. We conclude that *Albrecht* should be overruled.

---

[18] 390 U.S. 145 (1968).

I

. . .

We . . . consider two questions, whether State Oil's conduct constitutes a per se violation of the Sherman Act and whether respondents are entitled to recover damages based on that conduct.

II

A

Although the Sherman Act, by its terms, prohibits every agreement "in restraint of trade," this Court has long recognized that Congress intended to outlaw only unreasonable restraints. As a consequence, most antitrust claims are analyzed under a "rule of reason," according to which the finder of fact must decide whether the questioned practice imposes an unreasonable restraint on competition, taking into account a variety of factors, including specific information about the relevant business, its condition before and after the restraint was imposed, and the restraint's history, nature, and effect.

Some types of restraints, however, have such predictable and pernicious anticompetitive effect, and such limited potential for procompetitive benefit, that they are deemed unlawful per se. Per se treatment is appropriate "[o]nce experience with a particular kind of restraint enables the Court to predict with confidence that the rule of reason will condemn it." Thus, we have expressed reluctance to adopt per se rules with regard to "restraints imposed in the context of business relationships where the economic impact of certain practices is not immediately obvious."

. . .

Albrecht . . . involved a newspaper publisher who had granted exclusive territories to independent carriers subject to their adherence to a maximum price on resale of the newspapers to the public. . . . [T]he Court concluded that it was per se unlawful for the publisher to fix the maximum resale price of its newspapers. The Court acknowledged that "[m]aximum and minimum price fixing may have different consequences in many situations," but nonetheless condemned maximum price fixing for "substituting the perhaps erroneous judgment of a seller for the forces of the competitive market."

Albrecht was animated in part by the fear that vertical maximum price fixing could allow suppliers to discriminate against certain dealers, restrict the services that dealers could afford to offer customers, or disguise minimum price fixing schemes. The Court rejected the notion (both on the record of that case and in the abstract) that, because the newspaper publisher "granted exclusive territories, a price ceiling was necessary to protect the public from price gouging by dealers who had monopoly power in their own territories."

. . .

B

Thus, our reconsideration of *Albrecht*'s continuing validity is informed by several of our decisions, as well as a considerable body of scholarship discussing the effects of vertical restraints. Our analysis is also guided by our general view that the primary purpose of the antitrust laws is to protect interbrand competition. "Low prices," we have explained, "benefit consumers regardless of how those prices are set, and so long as they are above predatory levels, they do not threaten competition." Our interpretation of the Sherman Act also incorporates the notion that condemnation of practices resulting in lower prices to consumers is "especially costly" because "cutting prices in order to increase business often is the very essence of competition."

So informed, we find it difficult to maintain that vertically-imposed maximum prices could harm consumers or competition to the extent necessary to justify their per se invalidation. . . .

We recognize that the *Albrecht* decision presented a number of theoretical justifications for a per se rule against vertical maximum price fixing. But criticism of those premises abounds. . . .

Not only are the potential injuries cited in *Albrecht* less serious than the Court imagined, the per se rule established therein could in fact exacerbate problems related to the unrestrained exercise of market power by monopolist-dealers. Indeed, both courts and antitrust scholars have noted that *Albrecht*'s rule may actually harm consumers and manufacturers. . . .

After reconsidering *Albrecht*'s rationale and the substantial criticism the decision has received, however, we conclude that there is insufficient economic justification for per se invalidation of vertical maximum price fixing. That is so not only because it is difficult to accept the assumptions underlying *Albrecht*, but also because *Albrecht* has little or no relevance to ongoing enforcement of the Sherman Act. Moreover, neither the parties nor any of the *amici curiae* have called our attention to any cases in which enforcement efforts have been directed solely against the conduct encompassed by *Albrecht*'s per se rule.

. . .

C

Despite what Chief Judge Posner aptly described as *Albrecht*'s "infirmities, [and] its increasingly wobbly, moth-eaten foundations," there remains the question whether *Albrecht* deserves continuing respect under the doctrine of *stare decisis*. . . .

We approach the reconsideration of decisions of this Court with the utmost caution. *Stare decisis* reflects "a policy judgment that 'in most matters it is more important that the applicable rule of law be settled than that it be settled right.'" It "is the preferred course because it promotes the evenhanded, predictable, and consistent development of legal principles, fosters reliance on judicial decisions, and contributes to the actual and perceived integrity of the judicial process." This Court has expressed its reluctance to overrule decisions involving statutory interpretation, and has acknowledged that *stare decisis* concerns are at their acme in cases involving property and contract rights. Both of those concerns are arguably relevant in this case.

But "[s]tare decisis is not an inexorable command." In the area of antitrust law, there is a competing interest, well-represented in this Court's decisions, in recognizing and adapting to changed circumstances and the lessons of accumulated experience. Thus, the general presumption that legislative changes should be left to Congress has less force with respect to the Sherman Act in light of the accepted view that Congress "expected the courts to give shape to the statute's broad mandate by drawing on common-law tradition." As we have explained, the term "restraint of trade," as used in §1, also "invokes the common law itself, and not merely the static content that the common law had assigned to the term in 1890." Accordingly, this Court has reconsidered its decisions construing the Sherman Act when the theoretical underpinnings of those decisions are called into serious question.

Although we do not "lightly assume that the economic realities underlying earlier decisions have changed, or that earlier judicial perceptions of those realities were in error," we have noted that "different sorts of agreements" may amount to restraints of trade "in varying times and circumstances," and "[i]t would make no sense to create out of the single term 'restraint of trade' a chronologically schizoid statute, in which a 'rule of reason' evolves with new circumstances and new wisdom, but a line of per se illegality remains forever fixed where it was. . . ."

Although the rule of *Albrecht* has been in effect for some time, the inquiry we must undertake requires considering "'the effect of the antitrust laws upon vertical distributional restraints in the American economy today.'" As the Court noted in *ARCO*,[19] there has not been another case since *Albrecht* in which this Court has "confronted an unadulterated vertical, maximum-price-fixing arrangement." Now that we confront *Albrecht* directly, we find its conceptual foundations gravely weakened.

In overruling *Albrecht*, we of course do not hold that all vertical maximum price fixing is per se lawful. Instead, vertical maximum price fixing, like the majority of commercial arrangements subject to the antitrust laws, should be evaluated under the rule of reason. In our view, rule-of-reason analysis will effectively identify those situations in which vertical maximum price fixing amounts to anticompetitive conduct.

There remains the question whether respondents are entitled to recover damages based on State Oil's conduct. Although the Court of Appeals noted that "the district judge was right to conclude that if the rule of reason is applicable, Khan loses," its consideration of this case was necessarily premised on *Albrecht*'s per se rule. Under the circumstances, the matter should be reviewed by the Court of Appeals in the first instance. We therefore vacate the judgment of the Court of Appeals and remand the case for further proceedings consistent with this opinion.

It is so ordered.

---

[19] Atlantic Richfield Co. v. USA Petroleum Co., 495 U.S. 328 (1990).

SHARON TAXMAN V. BOARD OF EDUCATION OF THE TOWNSHIP OF PISCATAWAY

UNITED STATES COURT OF APPEALS FOR THE THIRD CIRCUIT

91 F.3d 1547

Decided Aug. 8, 1996
As Amended Aug. 21, 1996

"[I]t is beyond cavil that the Board, by invoking its affirmative action policy to lay off Sharon Taxman, violated the terms of Title VII. . . . [T]he Board must justify its deviation from the statutory mandate based on positive legislative history, not on its idea of what is appropriate."

Background: The United States brought a Title VII action challenging the Piscataway school board's affirmative action plan, which gave preferences to minority teachers over nonminority teachers in layoff decisions when teachers were equally qualified. Sharon Taxman, a white teacher who had been laid off, intervened as a plaintiff and asserted claims under Title VII and the New Jersey Law Against Discrimination (NJLAD). The Federal District Court entered summary judgment for the United States and Taxman. The District Court awarded Taxman damages for backpay, fringe benefits, and prejudgment interest under Title VII but dismissed her claim for punitive damages. Taxman and the school board appealed.

Held: The Piscataway school board's challenged affirmative action policy violated Title VII and the NJLAD. [*Eds.*: The U.S. Supreme Court agreed to hear this case during the 1997–1998 term.]

Opinion: By MANSMANN, Circuit Judge.

In this Title VII matter, we must determine whether the Board of Education of the Township of Piscataway violated that statute when it made race a factor in selecting which of two equally qualified employees to lay off. Specifically, we must decide whether Title VII permits an employer with a racially balanced work force to grant a non-remedial racial preference in order to promote "racial diversity."

It is clear that the language of Title VII is violated when an employer makes an employment decision based upon an employee's race. The Supreme Court determined in *United Steelworkers v. Weber*,[20] however, that Title VII's prohibition against racial discrimination is not violated by affirmative action plans which first, "have purposes that mirror those of the statute" and second, do not "unnecessarily trammel the interests of the [non-minority] employees."

---

[20] 443 U.S. 193 (1979).

We hold that Piscataway's affirmative action policy is unlawful because it fails to satisfy either prong of *Weber*. Given the clear antidiscrimination mandate of Title VII, a non-remedial affirmative action plan, even one with a laudable purpose, cannot pass muster. We will affirm the district court's grant of summary judgment to Sharon Taxman.

I.

In 1975, the Board of Education of the Township of Piscataway, New Jersey, developed an affirmative action policy applicable to employment decisions. The Board's Affirmative Action Program, a 52-page document, was originally adopted in response to a regulation promulgated by the New Jersey State Board of Education. That regulation directed local school boards to adopt "affirmative action programs," to address employment as well as school and classroom practices and to ensure equal opportunity to all persons regardless of race, color, creed, religion, sex or national origin. In 1983 the Board also adopted a one page "Policy," entitled "Affirmative Action—Employment Practices." It is not clear from the record whether the "Policy" superseded or simply added to the "Program," nor does it matter for purposes of this appeal.

The 1975 document states that the purpose of the Program is "to provide equal educational opportunity for students and equal employment opportunity for employees and prospective employees," and "to make a concentrated effort to attract . . . minority personnel for all positions so that their qualifications can be evaluated along with other candidates." The 1983 document states that its purpose is to "ensure[ ] equal employment opportunity . . . and prohibit [ ] discrimination in employment because of [, inter alia,] race. . . ."

The operative language regarding the means by which affirmative-action goals are to be furthered is identical in the two documents. "In all cases, the most qualified candidate will be recommended for appointment. However, when candidates appear to be of equal qualification, candidates meeting the criteria of the affirmative action program will be recommended." The phrase "candidates meeting the criteria of the affirmative action program" refers to members of racial, national origin or gender groups identified as minorities for statistical reporting purposes by the New Jersey State Department of Education, including Blacks. The 1983 document also clarifies that the affirmative action program applies to "every aspect of employment including . . . layoffs. . . ."

The Board's affirmative action policy did not have "any remedial purpose"; it was not adopted "with the intention of remedying the results of any prior discrimination or identified underrepresentation of minorities within the Piscataway Public School System." At all relevant times, Black teachers were neither "underrepresented" nor "underutilized" in the Piscataway School District work force. Indeed, statistics in 1976 and 1985 showed that the percentage of Black employees in the job category which included teachers exceeded the percentage of Blacks in the available work force.

A

In May, 1989, the Board accepted a recommendation from the Superintendent of Schools to reduce the teaching staff in the Business Department at Piscataway High School by one. At that time, two of the teachers in the department were of equal seniority, both having begun their employment with the Board on the same day nine years earlier. One of those teachers was intervenor plaintiff Sharon Taxman, who is White, and the other was Debra Williams, who is Black. Williams was the only minority teacher among the faculty of the Business Department.

Decisions regarding layoffs by New Jersey school boards are highly circumscribed by state law; nontenured faculty must be laid off first, and layoffs among tenured teachers in the affected subject area or grade level must proceed in reverse order of seniority. Seniority for this purpose is calculated according to specific guidelines set by state law. Thus, local boards lack discretion to choose between employees for layoff, except in the rare instance of a tie in seniority between the two or more employees eligible to fill the last remaining position.

The Board determined that it was facing just such a rare circumstance in deciding between Taxman and Williams. In prior decisions involving the layoff of employees with equal seniority, the Board had broken the tie through "a random process which included drawing numbers out of a container, drawing lots or having a lottery." In none of those instances, however, had the employees involved been of different races.

In light of the unique posture of the layoff decision, Superintendent of Schools Burton Edelchick recommended to the Board that the affirmative action plan be invoked in order to determine which teacher to retain. Superintendent Edelchick made this recommendation "because he believed Ms. Williams and Ms. Taxman were tied in seniority, were equally qualified, and because Ms. Williams was the only Black teacher in the Business Education Department."

While the Board recognized that it was not bound to apply the affirmative action policy, it made a discretionary decision to invoke the policy to break the tie between Williams and Taxman. As a result, the Board "voted to terminate the employment of Sharon Taxman, effective June 30, 1988. . . ."

. . .

B

. . .

II.

In relevant part, Title VII makes it unlawful for an employer "to discriminate against any individual with respect to his compensation, terms, conditions, or privileges of employment" or "to limit, segregate, or classify his employees . . . in any way which would deprive or tend to deprive any individual of employment opportunities or otherwise affect his status as an employee" on the basis of "race, color, religion, sex, or national origin." For a time, the Supreme Court construed this language as absolutely prohibiting discrimination in employment, neither requiring nor permitting any preference for any group.

In 1979, however, the Court interpreted the statute's "antidiscriminatory strategy" in a "fundamentally different way" holding in the seminal case of *United Steelworkers v. Weber* that Title VII's prohibition against racial discrimination does not condemn all voluntary race-conscious affirmative action plans.

. . .

. . . The [*Weber*] Court . . . embarked upon an exhaustive review of Title VII's legislative history and identified Congress' concerns in enacting Title VII's prohibition against discrimination—the deplorable status of Blacks in the nation's economy, racial injustice, and the need to open employment opportunities for Blacks in traditionally closed occupations. Against this background, the Court concluded that Congress could not have intended to prohibit private employers from implementing programs directed toward the very goal of Title VII—the eradication of discrimination and its effects from the workplace. . . .

. . .

III.

. . .

IV.

Having reviewed the analytical framework for assessing the validity of an affirmative action plan as established in *United Steelworkers v. Weber* and refined in [*Johnson v. Transportation Agency*],[21] we turn to the facts of this case in order to determine whether the racial diversity purpose of the Board's policy mirrors the purposes of the statute. We look for the purposes of Title VII in the plain meaning of the Act's provisions and in its legislative history and historical context.

A

Title VII was enacted to further two primary goals: to end discrimination on the basis of race, color, religion, sex or national origin, thereby guaranteeing equal opportunity in the workplace, and to remedy the segregation and underrepresentation of minorities that discrimination has caused in our Nation's work force.

Title VII's first purpose is set forth in section 2000e-2's several prohibitions, which expressly denounce the discrimination which Congress sought to end. This antidiscriminatory purpose is also reflected in the Act's legislative history. . . .

Title VII's second purpose, ending the segregative effects of discrimination, is revealed in the congressional debate surrounding the statute's enactment. . . .

The significance of this second corrective purpose cannot be overstated. It is only because Title VII was written to eradicate not only discrimination per se but the consequences of prior discrimination as well, that racial preferences in the form of affirmative action can co-exist with the Act's antidiscrimination mandate.

Thus, based on our analysis of Title VII's two goals, we are convinced that unless an affirmative action plan has a remedial purpose, it cannot be said to mirror the purposes of the statute, and, therefore, cannot satisfy the first prong of the *Weber* test.

We see this case as one involving straightforward statutory interpretation controlled by the text and legislative history of Title VII as interpreted in *Weber* and *Johnson*. The statute on its face provides that race cannot be a factor in employer decisions about hires, promotions, and layoffs, and the legislative history demonstrates that barring considerations of race from the workplace was Congress' primary objective. If exceptions to this bar are to be made, they must be made on the basis of what Congress has said. The affirmative action plans at issue in *Weber* and *Johnson* were sustained only because the Supreme Court, examining those plans in light of congressional intent, found a secondary congressional objective in Title VII that had to be accommodated—i.e., the elimination of the effects of past discrimination in the workplace. Here, there is no congressional recognition of diversity as a Title VII objective requiring accommodation.

Accordingly, it is beyond cavil that the Board, by invoking its affirmative action policy to lay off Sharon Taxman, violated the terms of Title VII. While the Court in *Weber* and *Johnson* permitted some deviation from the antidiscrimination mandate of the statute in order to erase the

---

[21] 480 U.S. 616 (1987).

effects of past discrimination, these rulings do not open the door to additional non-remedial deviations. Here, as in *Weber* and *Johnson*, the Board must justify its deviation from the statutory mandate based on positive legislative history, not on its idea of what is appropriate.

B

The Board recognizes that there is no positive legislative history supporting its goal of promoting racial diversity "for education's sake," and concedes that there is no caselaw approving such a purpose to support an affirmative action plan under Title VII. . . .

. . .

V.

Since we have not found anything in the Board's arguments to convince us that this case requires examination beyond statutory interpretation, we return to the point at which we started: the language of Title VII itself and the two cases reviewing affirmative action plans in light of that statute. Our analysis of the statute and the caselaw convinces us that a non-remedial affirmative action plan cannot form the basis for deviating from the antidiscrimination mandate of Title VII.

The Board admits that it did not act to remedy the effects of past employment discrimination. The parties have stipulated that neither the Board's adoption of its affirmative action policy nor its subsequent decision to apply it in choosing between Taxman and Williams was intended to remedy the results of any prior discrimination or identified underrepresentation of Blacks within the Piscataway School District's teacher workforce as a whole. Nor does the Board contend that its action here was directed at remedying any de jure or de facto segregation. Even though the Board's race-conscious action was taken to avoid what could have been an all-White faculty within the Business Department, the Board concedes that Blacks are not underrepresented in its teaching workforce as a whole or even in the Piscataway High School.

Rather, the Board's sole purpose in applying its affirmative action policy in this case was to obtain an educational benefit which it believed would result from a racially diverse faculty. While the benefits flowing from diversity in the educational context are significant indeed, we are constrained to hold, as did the district court, that inasmuch as "the Board does not even attempt to show that its affirmative action plan was adopted to remedy past discrimination or as the result of a manifest imbalance in the employment of minorities," the Board has failed to satisfy the first prong of the *Weber* test.

We turn next to the second prong of the *Weber* analysis. This second prong requires that we determine whether the Board's policy "unnecessarily trammel[s] ... [nonminority] interests. . . ." Under this requirement, too, the Board's policy is deficient.

We begin by noting the policy's utter lack of definition and structure. While it is not for us to decide how much diversity in a high school facility is "enough," the Board cannot abdicate its responsibility to define "racial diversity" and to determine what degree of racial diversity in the Piscataway School is sufficient.

The affirmative action plans that have met with the Supreme Court's approval under Title VII had objectives, as well as benchmarks which served to evaluate progress, guide the employment decisions at issue and assure the grant of only those minority preferences necessary to further the plans' purpose. By contrast, the Board's policy, devoid of goals and standards, is governed entirely by the Board's whim, leaving the Board free, if it so chooses, to grant racial preferences that do not promote even the policy's claimed purpose. Indeed, under the terms of this policy, the Board, in pursuit of a "racially diverse" work force, could use affirmative action to discriminate against those whom Title VII was enacted to protect. Such a policy unnecessarily trammels the interests of nonminority employees.

Moreover, both *Weber* and *Johnson* unequivocally provide that valid affirmative action plans are "temporary" measures that seek to "'attain'", not "maintain" a "permanent racial . . . balance." The Board's policy, adopted in 1975, is an established fixture of unlimited duration, to be resurrected from time to time whenever the Board believes that the ratio between Blacks and Whites in any Piscataway School is skewed. On this basis alone, the policy contravenes *Weber's* teaching.

Finally, we are convinced that the harm imposed upon a nonminority employee by the loss of his or her job is so substantial and the cost so severe that the Board's goal of racial diversity, even if legitimate under Title VII, may not be pursued in this particular fashion. This is especially true where, as here, the nonminority employee is tenured. In *Weber* and *Johnson*, when considering whether nonminorities were unduly encumbered by affirmative action, the Court found it significant that they retained their employment. We, therefore, adopt the plurality's pronouncement in *Wygant* that "[w]hile hiring goals impose a diffuse burden, often foreclosing only one of several opportunities, layoffs impose the entire burden of achieving racial equality on particular individuals, often resulting in serious disruption of their lives. That burden is too intrusive."

Accordingly, we conclude that under the second prong of the *Weber* test, the Board's affirmative action policy violates Title VII. In addition to containing an impermissible purpose, the policy "unnecessarily trammel[s] the interests of the [nonminority] employees."

VI.

The district court did not analyze Taxman's claims based on the New Jersey Law Against Discrimination and we need not do so in detail here. The parties have agreed that the legal analysis required by the state statute is essentially the same as that undertaken in Title VII cases. While the New Jersey Supreme Court has yet to consider a voluntarily adopted affirmative action plan in light of the NJLAD, it is undisputed that the NJLAD has been interpreted to parallel Title VII. . . .

VII.

. . .

VIII.

While we have rejected the argument that the Board's non-remedial application of the affirmative action policy is consistent with the language and intent of Title VII, we do not reject in principle the diversity goal articulated by the Board. Indeed, we recognize that the differences among us underlie the richness and strength of our Nation. Our disposition of this matter, however, rests squarely on the foundation of Title VII. Although we applaud the goal of racial diversity, we cannot agree that Title VII permits an employer to advance that goal through non-remedial discriminatory measures.

Having found that the district court properly concluded that the affirmative action plan applied by the Board to lay off Taxman is invalid under Title VII, and that the district court did not err in calculating Taxman's damages or in dismissing her claim for punitive damages, we will affirm the judgment of the district court.

Dissent: SLOVITER, Chief Judge, dissenting.

In the law, as in other professions, it is often how the question is framed that determines the answer that is received. Although the divisive issue of affirmative action continues on this country's political agenda, I do not see this appeal as raising a broad legal referendum on affirmative action policies. Indeed, it is questionable whether this case is about affirmative action at all, as that term has come to be generally understood—i.e. preference based on race or gender of one deemed "less qualified" over one deemed "more qualified." Nor does this case even require us to examine the parameters of the affirmative action policy originally adopted in 1975 by the Board of Education of the Township of Piscataway (School Board or Board) in response to a state regulation requiring affirmative action programs or the Board's concise 1983 one-page Affirmative Action policy.

Instead, the narrow question posed by this appeal can be restated as whether Title VII requires a New Jersey school or school board, which is faced with deciding which of two equally qualified teachers should be laid off, to make its decision through a coin toss or lottery, a solution that could be expected of the state's gaming tables, or whether Title VII permits the school board to factor into the decision its bona fide belief, based on its experience with secondary schools, that students derive educational benefit by having a Black faculty member in an otherwise all-White department. Because I believe that the area of discretion left to employers in educational institutions by Title VII encompasses the School Board's action in this case, I respectfully dissent.

. . .

Dissent: SCIRICA, Circuit Judge, dissenting.

While I find much with which I agree in the majority's opinion, I am constrained to express my disagreement because I believe education presents unique concerns.

. . .

In this case, the Piscataway Board of Education concluded that a diverse faculty . . . serves a compelling educational purpose; namely, it benefits students in the business department by exposing them to teachers with varied backgrounds. The Board implemented a program that, in limited circumstances, allows consideration of race as a factor in school employment decisions. The Board did not countenance the layoff of a more-qualified teacher in the place of a less-qualified one. It did not prefer teachers junior in seniority to those with more experience. Rather it concluded that when teachers are equal in ability and in all other respects—and only then—diversity of the faculty is a relevant consideration.

I do not believe Title VII prevents a school district, in the exercise of its professional judgment, from preferring one equally qualified teacher over another for a valid educational purpose.

Accordingly, I respectfully dissent.

Dissent: LEWIS, Circuit Judge, dissenting.

I join in Chief Judge Sloviter's dissent, as well as those of each of my dissenting colleagues.

I would only add that we should be mindful of the effects the majority's approach will impose upon legitimate, thoughtful efforts to redress the vestiges of our Nation's history of discrimination in the workplace and in education; efforts which, in seeking to achieve pluralism and diversity, have helped define and enrich our offices and institutions, and which were intended to open, and keep open, the doors of opportunity to those who have "been excluded from the American dream for so long." This, after all, is what I had always thought Title VII was intended to accomplish. More importantly, as Chief Judge Sloviter notes, these goals are plainly supported by the statute's legislative history. Thus, while the majority holds that Title VII only allows race to be considered in remedying a history of intentional discrimination or a "manifest imbalance," I believe this conclusion is fundamentally at odds with the overriding goals of the statute. . . .

. . .

. . . I believe the majority's decision eviscerates the purpose and the goals of Title VII. I respectfully dissent.

Dissent: McKEE, Circuit Judge, dissenting.

. . .

We have now come full circle. A law enacted by Congress in 1964 to move this country closer to an integrated society and away from the legacy of "separate but equal" is being interpreted as outlawing this Board of Education's good faith effort to teach students the value of diversity. The selection of Ms. Williams meant that the business department would retain the only Black teacher tenured in that department in anyone's memory. . . .

. . .

. . . I respectfully dissent.

Amended Judgment

This cause came on to be heard on the record from the United States District Court for the District of New Jersey and was argued by counsel November 29, 1995, and reargued before the Court in banc May 14, 1996.

On consideration whereof, it is now here ordered and adjudged by this Court that the judgment of the said District Court entered February 15, 1994, be, and the same is hereby affirmed. . . . All of the above in accordance with the opinion of this Court.

UNITED STATES V. ALFONSO LOPEZ, JR.

SUPREME COURT OF THE UNITED STATES

115 S. Ct. 1624

Decided April 26, 1995

"Under the theories that the Government presents in support of § 922(q) [which banned carrying guns in school zones], it is difficult to perceive any limitation on federal power, even in areas such as criminal law enforcement or education where States historically have been sovereign. Thus, if we were to accept the Government's arguments, we are hard-pressed to posit any activity by an individual that Congress is without power to regulate."

Background: After Alfonso Lopez, Jr. (Lopez), then a 12th-grade student, carried a concealed handgun into his high school, he was charged with violating the Federal Gun-Free School Zones Act of 1990. Section 922(q) of the act forbids "any individual knowingly to possess a firearm at a place that [he] knows . . . is a school zone." The Federal District Court denied Lopez's motion to dismiss the indictment, concluding that Section 922(q) was a constitutional exercise of Congress' power to regulate activities in and affecting interstate commerce. In reversing, the U.S. Court of Appeals held that, in light of what it characterized as insufficient congressional findings and legislative history, Section 922(q) was invalid as beyond the power of Congress under the Commerce Clause. The United States appealed.

Held: Section 922(q) exceeded Congress' authority to regulate interstate commerce under the Commerce Clause, and is therefore unconstitutional.

Opinion: Chief Justice REHNQUIST delivered the opinion of the Court.

. . .

We start with first principles. The Constitution creates a Federal Government of enumerated powers. As James Madison wrote, "[t]he powers delegated by the proposed Constitution to the federal government are few and defined. Those which are to remain in the State governments are numerous and indefinite." This constitutionally mandated division of authority "was adopted by the Framers to ensure protection of our fundamental liberties." "Just as the separation and independence of the coordinate branches of the Federal Government serves to prevent the accumulation of excessive power in any one branch, a healthy balance of power between the States and the Federal Government will reduce the risk of tyranny and abuse from either front."

The Constitution delegates to Congress the power "[t]o regulate Commerce with foreign Nations, and among the several States, and with the Indian Tribes." The Court, through Chief Justice Marshall, first defined the nature of Congress' commerce power in *Gibbons v. Ogden*:[22]

---

[22] 22 U.S. 1 (1824).

Commerce, undoubtedly, is traffic, but it is something more: it is intercourse. It describes the commercial intercourse between nations, and parts of nations, in all its branches, and is regulated by prescribing rules for carrying on that intercourse.

The commerce power "is the power to regulate; that is, to prescribe the rule by which commerce is to be governed. This power, like all others vested in Congress, is complete in itself, may be exercised to its utmost extent, and acknowledges no limitations, other than are prescribed in the constitution." The *Gibbons* Court, however, acknowledged that limitations on the commerce power are inherent in the very language of the Commerce Clause.

It is not intended to say that these words comprehend that commerce, which is completely internal, which is carried on between man and man in a State, or between different parts of the same State, and which does not extend to or affect other States. Such a power would be inconvenient, and is certainly unnecessary.

Comprehensive as the word 'among' is, it may very properly be restricted to that commerce which concerns more States than one.... The enumeration presupposes something not enumerated; and that something, if we regard the language or the subject of the sentence, must be the exclusively internal commerce of a State.

For nearly a century thereafter, the Court's Commerce Clause decisions dealt but rarely with the extent of Congress' power, and almost entirely with the Commerce Clause as a limit on state legislation that discriminated against interstate commerce. Under this line of precedent, the Court held that certain categories of activity such as "production," "manufacturing," and "mining" were within the province of state governments, and thus were beyond the power of Congress under the Commerce Clause.

In 1887, Congress enacted the Interstate Commerce Act, and in 1890, Congress enacted the Sherman Antitrust Act. These laws ushered in a new era of federal regulation under the commerce power. When cases involving these laws first reached this Court, we imported from our negative Commerce Clause cases the approach that Congress could not regulate activities such as "production," "manufacturing," and "mining." Simultaneously, however, the Court held that, where the interstate and intrastate aspects of commerce were so mingled together that full regulation of interstate commerce required incidental regulation of intrastate commerce, the Commerce Clause authorized such regulation.

. . .

. . . [I]n the watershed case of *NLRB v. Jones & Laughlin Steel Corp.*,[23] the Court upheld the National Labor Relations Act against a Commerce Clause challenge, and in the process, departed from the distinction between "direct" and "indirect" effects on interstate commerce. The Court held that intrastate activities that "have such a close and substantial relation to interstate commerce that their control is essential or appropriate to protect that commerce from burdens and obstructions" are within Congress' power to regulate.

. . .

Jones & Laughlin Steel . . . ushered in an era of Commerce Clause jurisprudence that greatly expanded the previously defined authority of Congress under that Clause. In part, this

---

[23] 301 U.S. 1 (1937).

was a recognition of the great changes that had occurred in the way business was carried on in this country. Enterprises that had once been local or at most regional in nature had become national in scope. But the doctrinal change also reflected a view that earlier Commerce Clause cases artificially had constrained the authority of Congress to regulate interstate commerce.

But even these modern-era precedents which have expanded congressional power under the Commerce Clause confirm that this power is subject to outer limits. In *Jones & Laughlin Steel*, the Court warned that the scope of the interstate commerce power "must be considered in the light of our dual system of government and may not be extended so as to embrace effects upon interstate commerce so indirect and remote that to embrace them, in view of our complex society, would effectually obliterate the distinction between what is national and what is local and create a completely centralized government." Since that time, the Court has heeded that warning and undertaken to decide whether a rational basis existed for concluding that a regulated activity sufficiently affected interstate commerce.

. . .

. . . [W]e have identified three broad categories of activity that Congress may regulate under its commerce power. First, Congress may regulate the use of the channels of interstate commerce. Second, Congress is empowered to regulate and protect the instrumentalities of interstate commerce, or persons or things in interstate commerce, even though the threat may come only from intrastate activities. Finally, Congress' commerce authority includes the power to regulate those activities having a substantial relation to interstate commerce, i.e., those activities that substantially affect interstate commerce.

Within this final category, admittedly, our case law has not been clear whether an activity must "affect" or "substantially affect" interstate commerce in order to be within Congress' power to regulate it under the Commerce Clause. . . . We conclude, consistent with the great weight of our case law, that the proper test requires an analysis of whether the regulated activity "substantially affects" interstate commerce.

We now turn to consider the power of Congress, in the light of this framework, to enact § 922(q). The first two categories of authority may be quickly disposed of: § 922(q) is not a regulation of the use of the channels of interstate commerce, nor is it an attempt to prohibit the interstate transportation of a commodity through the channels of commerce; nor can § 922(q) be justified as a regulation by which Congress has sought to protect an instrumentality of interstate commerce or a thing in interstate commerce. Thus, if § 922(q) is to be sustained, it must be under the third category as a regulation of an activity that substantially affects interstate commerce.

First, we have upheld a wide variety of congressional Acts regulating intrastate economic activity where we have concluded that the activity substantially affected interstate commerce. . . .

Section 922(q) is a criminal statute that by its terms has nothing to do with "commerce" or any sort of economic enterprise, however broadly one might define those terms. Section 922(q) is not an essential part of a larger regulation of economic activity, in which the regulatory scheme could be undercut unless the intrastate activity were regulated. It cannot, therefore, be sustained under our cases upholding regulations of activities that arise out of or are connected with a commercial transaction, which viewed in the aggregate, substantially affects interstate commerce.

Second, § 922(q) contains no jurisdictional element which would ensure, through case-by-case inquiry, that the firearm possession in question affects interstate commerce. . . . [Section] 922(q) has no express jurisdictional element which might limit its reach to a discrete set of firearm possessions that additionally have an explicit connection with or effect on interstate commerce.

Although as part of our independent evaluation of constitutionality under the Commerce Clause we of course consider legislative findings, and indeed even congressional committee findings, regarding effect on interstate commerce, the Government concedes that "[n]either the statute nor its legislative history contain[s] express congressional findings regarding the effects upon interstate commerce of gun possession in a school zone." We agree with the Government that Congress normally is not required to make formal findings as to the substantial burdens that an activity has on interstate commerce. But to the extent that congressional findings would enable us to evaluate the legislative judgment that the activity in question substantially affected interstate commerce, even though no such substantial effect was visible to the naked eye, they are lacking here.

. . .

The Government's essential contention, in fine, is that we may determine here that § 922(q) is valid because possession of a firearm in a local school zone does indeed substantially affect interstate commerce. The Government argues that possession of a firearm in a school zone may result in violent crime and that violent crime can be expected to affect the functioning of the national economy in two ways. First, the costs of violent crime are substantial, and, through the mechanism of insurance, those costs are spread throughout the population. Second, violent crime reduces the willingness of individuals to travel to areas within the country that are perceived to be unsafe. The Government also argues that the presence of guns in schools poses a substantial threat to the educational process by threatening the learning environment. A handicapped educational process, in turn, will result in a less productive citizenry. That, in turn, would have an adverse effect on the Nation's economic well-being. As a result, the Government argues that Congress could rationally have concluded that § 922(q) substantially affects interstate commerce.

We pause to consider the implications of the Government's arguments. The Government admits, under its "costs of crime" reasoning, that Congress could regulate not only all violent crime, but all activities that might lead to violent crime, regardless of how tenuously they relate to interstate commerce. Similarly, under the Government's "national productivity" reasoning, Congress could regulate any activity that it found was related to the economic productivity of individual citizens: family law (including marriage, divorce, and child custody), for example. Under the theories that the Government presents in support of § 922(q), it is difficult to perceive any limitation on federal power, even in areas such as criminal law enforcement or education where States historically have been sovereign. Thus, if we were to accept the Government's arguments, we are hard-pressed to posit any activity by an individual that Congress is without power to regulate.

. . .

To uphold the Government's contentions here, we would have to pile inference upon inference in a manner that would bid fair to convert congressional authority under the Commerce Clause to a general police power of the sort retained by the States. Admittedly, some of our prior cases have taken long steps down that road, giving great deference to congressional action. The broad language in these opinions has suggested the possibility of additional expansion, but we decline here to proceed any further. To do so would require us to conclude that the Constitution's enumeration of powers does not presuppose something not enumerated and that there never will be a distinction between what is truly national and what is truly local. This we are unwilling to do.

For the foregoing reasons the judgment of the Court of Appeals is affirmed.

Concurrence: Justice KENNEDY, concurring.

The history of the judicial struggle to interpret the Commerce Clause during the transition from the economic system the Founders knew to the single, national market still emergent in our own era counsels great restraint before the Court determines that the Clause is insufficient to support an exercise of the national power. That history gives me some pause about today's decision, but I join the Court's opinion with these observations on what I conceive to be its necessary though limited holding.

. . .

The history of our Commerce Clause decisions contains at least two lessons of relevance to this case. The first, as stated at the outset, is the imprecision of content-based boundaries used without more to define the limits of the Commerce Clause. The second, related to the first but of even greater consequence, is that the Court as an institution and the legal system as a whole have an immense stake in the stability of our Commerce Clause jurisprudence as it has evolved to this point. . . .

. . .

The statute before us upsets the federal balance to a degree that renders it an unconstitutional assertion of the commerce power, and our intervention is required. As THE CHIEF JUSTICE explains, unlike the earlier cases to come before the Court here neither the actors nor their conduct have a commercial character, and neither the purposes nor the design of the statute have an evident commercial nexus. The statute makes the simple possession of a gun within 1,000 feet of the grounds of the school a criminal offense. In a sense any conduct in this interdependent world of ours has an ultimate commercial origin or consequence, but we have not yet said the commerce power may reach so far. If Congress attempts that extension, then at the least we must inquire whether the exercise of national power seeks to intrude upon an area of traditional state concern.

An interference of these dimensions occurs here, for it is well established that education is a traditional concern of the States. . . .

While it is doubtful that any State, or indeed any reasonable person, would argue that it is wise policy to allow students to carry guns on school premises, considerable disagreement exists about how best to accomplish that goal. In this circumstance, the theory and utility of our federalism are revealed, for the States may perform their role as laboratories for experimentation to devise various solutions where the best solution is far from clear.

. . .

The statute now before us forecloses the States from experimenting and exercising their own judgment in an area to which States lay claim by right of history and expertise, and it does so by regulating an activity beyond the realm of commerce in the ordinary and usual sense of that term. . . .

. . .

For these reasons, I join in the opinion and judgment of the Court.

Concurrence: Justice THOMAS, concurring.

The Court today properly concludes that the Commerce Clause does not grant Congress the authority to prohibit gun possession within 1,000 feet of a school, as it attempted to do in the Gun-Free School Zones Act of 1990. Although I join the majority, I write separately to observe that our case law has drifted far from the original understanding of the Commerce Clause. In a future case, we ought to temper our Commerce Clause jurisprudence in a manner that both makes sense of our more recent case law and is more faithful to the original understanding of that Clause.

. . .

Dissent: Justice STEVENS, dissenting.

The welfare of our future "Commerce with foreign Nations, and among the several States" is vitally dependent on the character of the education of our children. I therefore agree entirely with Justice BREYER's explanation of why Congress has ample power to prohibit the possession of firearms in or near schools—just as it may protect the school environment from harms posed by controlled substances such as asbestos or alcohol. I also agree with Justice SOUTER's exposition of the radical character of the Court's holding and its kinship with the discredited, pre-Depression version of substantive due process. I believe, however, that the Court's extraordinary decision merits this additional comment.

Guns are both articles of commerce and articles that can be used to restrain commerce. Their possession is the consequence, either directly or indirectly, of commercial activity. In my judgment, Congress' power to regulate commerce in firearms includes the power to prohibit possession of guns at any location because of their potentially harmful use; it necessarily follows that Congress may also prohibit their possession in particular markets. The market for the possession of handguns by school-age children is, distressingly, substantial. Whether or not the national interest in eliminating that market would have justified federal legislation in 1789, it surely does today.

Dissent: Justice SOUTER, dissenting.

In reviewing congressional legislation under the Commerce Clause, we defer to what is often a merely implicit congressional judgment that its regulation addresses a subject substantially affecting interstate commerce "if there is any rational basis for such a finding." If that congressional determination is within the realm of reason, "the only remaining question for judicial inquiry is whether 'the means chosen by Congress [are] reasonably adapted to the end permitted by the Constitution.'"

The practice of deferring to rationally based legislative judgments "is a paradigm of judicial restraint." In judicial review under the Commerce Clause, it reflects our respect for the institutional competence of the Congress on a subject expressly assigned to it by the Constitution and our appreciation of the legitimacy that comes from Congress's political accountability in dealing with matters open to a wide range of possible choices.

It was not ever thus, however, as even a brief overview of Commerce Clause history during the past century reminds us. The modern respect for the competence and primacy of Congress in matters affecting commerce developed only after one of this Court's most chastening experiences, when it perforce repudiated an earlier and untenably expansive conception of judicial review in derogation of congressional commerce power. A look at history's sequence will serve to show how today's decision tugs the Court off course, leading it to suggest opportunities for further developments that would be at odds with the rule of restraint to which the Court still wisely states adherence.

. . .

Dissent: Justice BREYER, dissenting.

The issue in this case is whether the Commerce Clause authorizes Congress to enact a statute that makes it a crime to possess a gun in, or near, a school. In my view, the statute falls well within the scope of the commerce power as this Court has understood that power over the last half-century.

I

In reaching this conclusion, I apply three basic principles of Commerce Clause interpretation. First, the power to "regulate Commerce . . . among the several States," encompasses the power to regulate local activities insofar as they significantly affect interstate commerce. . . .

Second, in determining whether a local activity will likely have a significant effect upon interstate commerce, a court must consider, not the effect of an individual act (a single instance of gun possession), but rather the cumulative effect of all similar instances (i.e., the effect of all guns possessed in or near schools). . . .

Third, the Constitution requires us to judge the connection between a regulated activity and interstate commerce, not directly, but at one remove. Courts must give Congress a degree of leeway in determining the existence of a significant factual connection between the regulated activity and interstate commerce—both because the Constitution delegates the commerce power directly to Congress and because the determination requires an empirical judgment of a kind that a legislature is more likely than a court to make with accuracy. The traditional words "rational basis" capture this leeway. Thus, the specific question before us, as the Court recognizes, is not whether the "regulated activity sufficiently affected interstate commerce," but, rather, whether Congress could have had "a rational basis" for so concluding.

. . .

II

Applying these principles to the case at hand, we must ask whether Congress could have had a rational basis for finding a significant (or substantial) connection between gun-related school violence and interstate commerce. Or, to put the question in the language of the explicit finding that Congress made when it amended this law in 1994: Could Congress rationally have found that "violent crime in school zones," through its effect on the "quality of education," significantly (or substantially) affects "interstate" or "foreign commerce"? As long as one views the commerce connection, not as a "technical legal conception," but as "a practical one," the answer to this question must be yes. Numerous reports and studies—generated both inside and outside government—make clear that Congress could reasonably have found the empirical connection that its law, implicitly or explicitly, asserts. . . .

For one thing, reports, hearings, and other readily available literature make clear that the problem of guns in and around schools is widespread and extremely serious. . . .

Having found that guns in schools significantly undermine the quality of education in our Nation's classrooms, Congress could also have found, given the effect of education upon interstate and foreign commerce, that gun-related violence in and around schools is a commercial, as well as a human, problem. . . .

In recent years the link between secondary education and business has strengthened, becoming both more direct and more important. . . .

Increasing global competition also has made primary and secondary education economically more important. . . .

Finally, there is evidence that, today more than ever, many firms base their location decisions upon the presence, or absence, of a work force with a basic education. . . .

The economic links I have just sketched seem fairly obvious. Why then is it not equally obvious, in light of those links, that a widespread, serious, and substantial physical threat to teaching and learning also substantially threatens the commerce to which that teaching and learning is inextricably tied? That is to say, guns in the hands of six percent of inner-city high school students and gun-related violence throughout a city's schools must threaten the trade and commerce that those schools support. The only question, then, is whether the latter threat is (to use the majority's terminology) "substantial." And, the evidence of (1) the extent of the gun-related violence problem, (2) the extent of the resulting negative effect on classroom learning, and (3) the extent of the consequent negative commercial effects, when taken together, indicate a threat to trade and commerce that is "substantial." At the very least, Congress could rationally have concluded that the links are "substantial."

. . .

In sum, a holding that the particular statute before us falls within the commerce power would not expand the scope of that Clause. Rather, it simply would apply preexisting law to changing economic circumstances. It would recognize that, in today's economic world, gun-related violence near the classroom makes a significant difference to our economic, as well as our social, well-being. In accordance with well-accepted precedent, such a holding would permit Congress "to act in terms of economic . . . realities," would interpret the commerce power as "an affirmative power commensurate with the national needs," and would acknowledge that the "commerce clause does not operate so as to render the nation powerless to defend itself against economic forces that Congress decrees inimical or destructive of the national economy."

. . .

UNITED STATES V. JAMES HERMAN O'HAGAN

SUPREME COURT OF THE UNITED STATES

117 S. Ct. 2199

Decided June 25, 1997

"Although informational disparity is inevitable in the securities markets, investors likely would hesitate to venture their capital in a market where trading based on misappropriated nonpublic information is unchecked by law. An investor's informational disadvantage vis-à-vis a misappropriator with material, nonpublic information stems from contrivance, not luck; it is a disadvantage that cannot be overcome with research or skill."

Background: Attorney James Herman O'Hagan purchased stock and options for stock in Pillsbury Company (Pillsbury) prior to the public announcement of a tender offer for Pillsbury's stock by Grand Met PLC (Grand Met). O'Hagan possessed material nonpublic information about Grand Met's intentions, which he had obtained as a partner of the law firm representing Grand Met in connection with its acquisition of Pillsbury. O'Hagan realized a profit in excess of $4,000,000 on his Pillsbury-related transactions.

The Securities and Exchange Commission (SEC) launched an investigation into O'Hagan's transactions, and he was criminally charged. O'Hagan was convicted of 57 counts of securities fraud, mail fraud, and money laundering. O'Hagan's securities fraud convictions were based on the misappropriation theory (which permits a securities fraud conviction based solely upon the misappropriation of material nonpublic information in breach of a fiduciary duty owed to the source of the information) and on Rule 14e-3(a) (which prohibits a person with nonpublic information about a tender offer from buying stock in the target company). O'Hagan appealed his conviction. The U.S. Court of Appeals reversed. It rejected the misappropriation theory, and held that O'Hagan had not committed securities fraud, because he did not owe a fiduciary duty to Pillsbury or its shareholders. It also struck down Rule 14e-3 after concluding that the SEC had exceeded its rulemaking authority. Because the Court of Appeals found that O'Hagan had not committed securities fraud, it also reversed the mail fraud and money laundering convictions. The United States appealed.

Held: A securities fraud conviction can be based on the misappropriation theory, and the SEC did not exceed its rulemaking authority in promulgating Rule 14e-3(a) with respect to cases involving misappropriation. Accordingly, O'Hagan was guilty of securities fraud, mail fraud, and money laundering.

Opinion: Justice GINSBURG delivered the opinion of the Court.

This case concerns the interpretation and enforcement of § 10(b) and § 14(e) of the Securities Exchange Act of 1934, and rules made by the Securities and Exchange Commission pursuant to these provisions, Rule 10b-5 and Rule 14e-3(a). Two prime questions are presented.

The first relates to the misappropriation of material, nonpublic information for securities trading; the second concerns fraudulent practices in the tender offer setting. In particular, we address and resolve these issues: (1) Is a person who trades in securities for personal profit, using confidential information misappropriated in breach of a fiduciary duty to the source of the information, guilty of violating § 10(b) and Rule 10b-5? (2) Did the Commission exceed its rulemaking authority by adopting Rule 14e-3(a), which proscribes trading on undisclosed information in the tender offer setting, even in the absence of a duty to disclose? Our answer to the first question is yes, and to the second question, viewed in the context of this case, no.

I

. . .

II

We address first the Court of Appeals' reversal of O'Hagan's convictions under § 10(b) and Rule 10b-5. Following the Fourth Circuit's lead, the Eighth Circuit rejected the misappropriation theory as a basis for § 10(b) liability. We hold, in accord with several other Courts of Appeals, that criminal liability under § 10(b) may be predicated on the misappropriation theory.

A

In pertinent part, § 10(b) of the Exchange Act provides:

> It shall be unlawful for any person, directly or indirectly, by the use of any means or instrumentality of interstate commerce or of the mails, or of any facility of any national securities exchange—

. . .

> (b) To use or employ, in connection with the purchase or sale of any security registered on a national securities exchange or any security not so registered, any manipulative or deceptive device or contrivance in contravention of such rules and regulations as the [Securities and Exchange] Commission may prescribe as necessary or appropriate in the public interest or for the protection of investors.

The statute thus proscribes (1) using any deceptive device (2) in connection with the purchase or sale of securities, in contravention of rules prescribed by the Commission. The provision, as written, does not confine its coverage to deception of a purchaser or seller of securities; rather, the statute reaches any deceptive device used "in connection with the purchase or sale of any security."

Pursuant to its § 10(b) rulemaking authority, the Commission has adopted Rule 10b-5, which, as relevant here, provides:

> It shall be unlawful for any person, directly or indirectly, by the use of any means or instrumentality of interstate commerce, or of the mails or of any facility of any national securities exchange,
> (a) To employ any device, scheme, or artifice to defraud, [or]

. . .

(c) To engage in any act, practice, or course of business which operates or would operate as a fraud or deceit upon any person, in connection with the purchase or sale of any security.

Liability under Rule 10b-5, our precedent indicates, does not extend beyond conduct encompassed by § 10(b)'s prohibition.

Under the "traditional" or "classical theory" of insider trading liability, § 10(b) and Rule 10b-5 are violated when a corporate insider trades in the securities of his corporation on the basis of material, nonpublic information. Trading on such information qualifies as a "deceptive device" under § 10(b), we have affirmed, because "a relationship of trust and confidence [exists] between the shareholders of a corporation and those insiders who have obtained confidential information by reason of their position with that corporation." That relationship, we recognized, "gives rise to a duty to disclose [or to abstain from trading] because of the 'necessity of preventing a corporate insider from . . . tak[ing] unfair advantage of . . . uninformed . . . stockholders.'" The classical theory applies not only to officers, directors, and other permanent insiders of a corporation, but also to attorneys, accountants, consultants, and others who temporarily become fiduciaries of a corporation.

The "misappropriation theory" holds that a person commits fraud "in connection with" a securities transaction, and thereby violates § 10(b) and Rule 10b-5, when he misappropriates confidential information for securities trading purposes, in breach of a duty owed to the source of the information. Under this theory, a fiduciary's undisclosed, self serving use of a principal's information to purchase or sell securities, in breach of a duty of loyalty and confidentiality, defrauds the principal of the exclusive use of that information. In lieu of premising liability on a fiduciary relationship between company insider and purchaser or seller of the company's stock, the misappropriation theory premises liability on a fiduciary turned trader's deception of those who entrusted him with access to confidential information.

The two theories are complementary, each addressing efforts to capitalize on nonpublic information through the purchase or sale of securities. The classical theory targets a corporate insider's breach of duty to shareholders with whom the insider transacts; the misappropriation theory outlaws trading on the basis of nonpublic information by a corporate "outsider" in breach of a duty owed not to a trading party, but to the source of the information. The misappropriation theory is thus designed to "protec[t] the integrity of the securities markets against abuses by 'outsiders' to a corporation who have access to confidential information that will affect th[e] corporation's security price when revealed, but who owe no fiduciary or other duty to that corporation's shareholders."

In this case, the indictment alleged that O'Hagan, in breach of a duty of trust and confidence he owed to his law firm, Dorsey & Whitney, and to its client, Grand Met, traded on the basis of nonpublic information regarding Grand Met's planned tender offer for Pillsbury common stock. This conduct, the Government charged, constituted a fraudulent device in connection with the purchase and sale of securities.

B

We agree with the Government that misappropriation, as just defined, satisfies § 10(b)'s requirement that chargeable conduct involve a "deceptive device or contrivance" used "in connection with" the purchase or sale of securities. We observe, first, that misappropriators, as the Government describes them, deal in deception. A fiduciary who "[pretends] loyalty to the principal while secretly converting the principal's information for personal gain" . . . defrauds the principal.

. . .

The misappropriation theory advanced by the Government is consistent with *Santa Fe Industries, Inc. v. Green*,[24] a decision underscoring that § 10(b) is not an all purpose breach of fiduciary duty ban; rather, it trains on conduct involving manipulation or deception. In contrast to the Government's allegations in this case, in *Santa Fe Industries*, all pertinent facts were disclosed by the persons charged with violating § 10(b) and Rule 10b-5; therefore, there was no deception through nondisclosure to which liability under those provisions could attach. Similarly, full disclosure forecloses liability under the misappropriation theory: Because the deception essential to the misappropriation theory involves feigning fidelity to the source of information, if the fiduciary discloses to the source that he plans to trade on the nonpublic information, there is no "deceptive device" and thus no § 10(b) violation—although the fiduciary turned trader may remain liable under state law for breach of a duty of loyalty.

We turn next to the § 10(b) requirement that the misappropriator's deceptive use of information be "in connection with the purchase or sale of [a] security." This element is satisfied because the fiduciary's fraud is consummated, not when the fiduciary gains the confidential information, but when, without disclosure to his principal, he uses the information to purchase or sell securities. The securities transaction and the breach of duty thus coincide. This is so even though the person or entity defrauded is not the other party to the trade, but is, instead, the source of the nonpublic information. A misappropriator who trades on the basis of material, nonpublic information, in short, gains his advantageous market position through deception; he deceives the source of the information and simultaneously harms members of the investing public.

. . .

The Government notes another limitation on the forms of fraud § 10(b) reaches: "The misappropriation theory would not . . . apply to a case in which a person defrauded a bank into giving him a loan or embezzled cash from another, and then used the proceeds of the misdeed to purchase securities." In such a case, the Government states, "the proceeds would have value to the malefactor apart from their use in a securities transaction, and the fraud would be complete as soon as the money was obtained." In other words, money can buy, if not anything, then at least many things; its misappropriation may thus be viewed as sufficiently detached from a subsequent securities transaction that § 10(b)'s "in connection with" requirement would not be met.

. . .

The misappropriation theory comports with § 10(b)'s language, which requires deception "in connection with the purchase or sale of any security," not deception of an identifiable purchaser or seller. The theory is also well tuned to an animating purpose of the Exchange Act: to insure honest securities markets and thereby promote investor confidence. Although informational disparity is inevitable in the securities markets, investors likely would hesitate to venture their capital in a market where trading based on misappropriated nonpublic information is unchecked by law. An investor's informational disadvantage vis-à-vis a misappropriator with material, nonpublic information stems from contrivance, not luck; it is a disadvantage that cannot be overcome with research or skill.

In sum, considering the inhibiting impact on market participation of trading on misappropriated information, and the congressional purposes underlying § 10(b), it makes scant sense to hold a lawyer like O'Hagan a § 10(b) violator if he works for a law firm representing the

---

[24] 430 U.S. 462 (1977).

target of a tender offer, but not if he works for a law firm representing the bidder. The text of the statute requires no such result. The misappropriation at issue here was properly made the subject of a § 10(b) charge because it meets the statutory requirement that there be "deceptive" conduct "in connection with" securities transactions.

. . .

III

We consider next the ground on which the Court of Appeals reversed O'Hagan's convictions for fraudulent trading in connection with a tender offer, in violation of § 14(e) of the Exchange Act and SEC Rule 14e-3(a). A sole question is before us as to these convictions: Did the Commission, as the Court of Appeals held, exceed its rulemaking authority under § 14(e) when it adopted Rule 14e-3(a) without requiring a showing that the trading at issue entailed a breach of fiduciary duty? We hold that the Commission, in this regard and to the extent relevant to this case, did not exceed its authority.

The governing statutory provision, § 14(e) of the Exchange Act, reads in relevant part:

It shall be unlawful for any person . . . to engage in any fraudulent, deceptive, or manipulative acts or practices, in connection with any tender offer. . . . The [SEC] shall, for the purposes of this subsection, by rules and regulations define, and prescribe means reasonably designed to prevent, such acts and practices as are fraudulent, deceptive, or manipulative.

Section 14(e)'s first sentence prohibits fraudulent acts in connection with a tender offer. This self operating proscription was one of several provisions added to the Exchange Act in 1968 by the Williams Act. The section's second sentence delegates definitional and prophylactic rule-making authority to the Commission. Congress added this rulemaking delegation to § 14(e) in 1970 amendments to the Williams Act.

Through § 14(e) and other provisions on disclosure in the Williams Act, Congress sought to ensure that shareholders "confronted by a cash tender offer for their stock [would] not be required to respond without adequate information." As we recognized in *Schreiber v. Burlington Northern, Inc.*,[25] Congress designed the Williams Act to make "disclosure, rather than court imposed principles of 'fairness' or 'artificiality,' . . . the preferred method of market regulation." Section 14(e), we explained, "supplements the more precise disclosure provisions found elsewhere in the Williams Act, while requiring disclosure more explicitly addressed to the tender offer context than that required by § 10(b)."

Relying on § 14(e)'s rulemaking authorization, the Commission, in 1980, promulgated Rule 14e-3(a). That measure provides:

(a) If any person has taken a substantial step or steps to commence, or has commenced, a tender offer (the 'offering person'), it shall constitute a fraudulent, deceptive or manipulative act or practice within the meaning of section 14(e) of the [Exchange] Act for any other person who is in possession of material information relating to such tender offer which information he knows or has reason to

---

[25] 472 U.S. 1 (1985).

know is nonpublic and which he knows or has reason to know has been acquired directly or indirectly from:

(1) The offering person,

(2) The issuer of the securities sought or to be sought by such tender offer, or

(3) Any officer, director, partner or employee or any other person acting on behalf of the offering person or such issuer, to purchase or sell or cause to be purchased or sold any of such securities or any securities convertible into or exchangeable for any such securities or any option or right to obtain or to dispose of any of the foregoing securities, unless within a reasonable time prior to any purchase or sale such information and its source are publicly disclosed by press release or otherwise.

As characterized by the Commission, Rule 14e-3(a) is a "disclose or abstain from trading" requirement. The Second Circuit concisely described the rule's thrust:

> One violates Rule 14e-3(a) if he trades on the basis of material nonpublic information concerning a pending tender offer that he knows or has reason to know has been acquired 'directly or indirectly' from an insider of the offeror or issuer, or someone working on their behalf. Rule 14e-3(a) is a disclosure provision. It creates a duty in those traders who fall within its ambit to abstain or disclose, without regard to whether the trader owes a pre-existing fiduciary duty to respect the confidentiality of the information.
>
> . . .

We need not resolve in this case whether the Commission's authority under § 14(e) to "define . . . such acts and practices as are fraudulent" is broader than the Commission's fraud defining authority under § 10(b), for we agree with the United States that Rule 14e-3(a), as applied to cases of this genre, qualifies under § 14(e) as a "means reasonably designed to prevent" fraudulent trading on material, nonpublic information in the tender offer context. A prophylactic measure, because its mission is to prevent, typically encompasses more than the core activity prohibited. As we noted in *Schreiber*, § 14(e)'s rulemaking authorization gives the Commission "latitude," even in the context of a term of art like "manipulative," "to regulate nondeceptive activities as a 'reasonably designed' means of preventing manipulative acts, without suggesting any change in the meaning of the term 'manipulative' itself." We hold, accordingly, that under § 14(e), the Commission may prohibit acts, not themselves fraudulent under the common law or § 10(b), if the prohibition is "reasonably designed to prevent . . . acts and practices [that] are fraudulent."

Because Congress has authorized the Commission, in § 14(e), to prescribe legislative rules, we owe the Commission's judgment "more than mere deference or weight." Therefore, in determining whether Rule 14e-3(a)'s "disclose or abstain from trading" requirement is reasonably designed to prevent fraudulent acts, we must accord the Commission's assessment "controlling weight unless [it is] arbitrary, capricious, or manifestly contrary to the statute." In this case, we conclude, the Commission's assessment is none of these.

In adopting the "disclose or abstain" rule, the SEC explained:

> The Commission has previously expressed and continues to have serious concerns about trading by persons in possession of material, nonpublic information relating to a tender offer. This practice results in unfair disparities in market information and market disruption. Security holders who purchase from or sell to such persons

are effectively denied the benefits of disclosure and the substantive protections of the Williams Act. If furnished with the information, these security holders would be able to make an informed investment decision, which could involve deferring the purchase or sale of the securities until the material information had been disseminated or until the tender offer has been commenced or terminated.

The Commission thus justified Rule 14e-3(a) as a means necessary and proper to assure the efficacy of Williams Act protections.

The United States emphasizes that Rule 14e-3(a) reaches trading in which "a breach of duty is likely but difficult to prove." "Particularly in the context of a tender offer," as the Tenth Circuit recognized, "there is a fairly wide circle of people with confidential information," notably, the attorneys, investment bankers, and accountants involved in structuring the transaction. The availability of that information may lead to abuse, for "even a hint of an upcoming tender offer may send the price of the target company's stock soaring." Individuals entrusted with nonpublic information, particularly if they have no long term loyalty to the issuer, may find the temptation to trade on that information hard to resist in view of "the very large short term profits potentially available [to them]."

"[I]t may be possible to prove circumstantially that a person [traded on the basis of material, nonpublic information], but almost impossible to prove that the trader obtained such information in breach of a fiduciary duty owed either by the trader or by the ultimate insider source of the information." The example of a "tippee" who trades on information received from an insider illustrates the problem. Under Rule 10b-5, "a tippee assumes a fiduciary duty to the shareholders of a corporation not to trade on material nonpublic information only when the insider has breached his fiduciary duty to the shareholders by disclosing the information to the tippee and the tippee knows or should know that there has been a breach." To show that a tippee who traded on nonpublic information about a tender offer had breached a fiduciary duty would require proof not only that the insider source breached a fiduciary duty, but that the tippee knew or should have known of that breach. "Yet, in most cases, the only parties to the [information transfer] will be the insider and the alleged tippee."

In sum, it is a fair assumption that trading on the basis of material, nonpublic information will often involve a breach of a duty of confidentiality to the bidder or target company or their representatives. The SEC, cognizant of the proof problem that could enable sophisticated traders to escape responsibility, placed in Rule 14e-3(a) a "disclose or abstain from trading" command that does not require specific proof of a breach of fiduciary duty. That prescription, we are satisfied, applied to this case, is a "means reasonably designed to prevent" fraudulent trading on material, nonpublic information in the tender offer context. Therefore, insofar as it serves to prevent the type of misappropriation charged against O'Hagan, Rule 14e-3(a) is a proper exercise of the Commission's prophylactic power under § 14(e).

. . .

IV

Based on its dispositions of the securities fraud convictions, the Court of Appeals also reversed O'Hagan's convictions, under 18 U.S.C. § 1341, for mail fraud. Reversal of the securities convictions, the Court of Appeals recognized, "d[id] not as a matter of law require that the mail fraud convictions likewise be reversed." But in this case, the Court of Appeals said, the indictment was so structured that the mail fraud charges could not be disassociated from the securities fraud charges, and absent any securities fraud, "there was no fraud upon which to base the mail fraud charges."

The United States urges that the Court of Appeals' position is irreconcilable with *Carpenter*:[26]   Just as in *Carpenter*, so here, the "mail fraud charges are independent of [the] securities fraud charges, even [though] both rest on the same set of facts."   We need not linger over this matter, for our rulings on the securities fraud issues require that we reverse the Court of Appeals judgment on the mail fraud counts as well.

O'Hagan, we note, attacked the mail fraud convictions in the Court of Appeals on alternate grounds; his other arguments, not yet addressed by the Eighth Circuit, remain open for consideration on remand.

* * *

The judgment of the Court of Appeals for the Eighth Circuit is reversed, and the case is remanded for further proceedings consistent with this opinion.

It is so ordered.

---

[26] *Carpenter v. United States*, 484 U.S. 19 (1987).

UNITED STATES V. GUY JEROME URSERY

UNITED STATES V. $405,089.23 IN UNITED STATES CURRENCY

Supreme Court of the United States

116 S. Ct. 2135

Decided June 24, 1996

"It is well settled that 'Congress may impose both a criminal and a civil sanction in respect to the same act or omission.' By itself, the fact that a forfeiture statute has some connection to a criminal violation is far from the 'clearest proof' necessary to show that a proceeding is criminal."

Background: In Case No. 95-345, Michigan police found marijuana growing adjacent to Guy Ursery's house, and discovered marijuana seeds, stems, stalks, and a growlight within the house. The United States instituted civil forfeiture proceedings against the house, alleging that the property was subject to forfeiture under a federal law (21 U.S.C. § 881(a)(7)) because it had been used for several years to facilitate the unlawful processing and distribution of a controlled substance. Ursery ultimately paid the United States $13,250 to settle the forfeiture claim in full. Shortly before the settlement was consummated, Ursery was criminally indicted for manufacturing marijuana, in violation of Section 841(a)(1) of 21 U.S.C. A jury found him guilty. The U.S. Court of Appeals reversed Ursery's criminal conviction, holding that the conviction violated the Double Jeopardy Clause of the United States Constitution.

In Case No. 95-346, Charles Wesley Arlt and James Wren were convicted of conspiracy to aid and abet the manufacture of methamphetamine, conspiracy to launder monetary instruments, and numerous counts of money laundering. Before the criminal trial had started, the United States had filed an in rem civil complaint (that is, an impersonal proceeding against property) against various items of property seized from, or titled to, Arlt and Wren, or Payback Mines, a corporation controlled by Arlt. The complaint alleged that each piece of property was subject to forfeiture under both 18 U.S.C. § 981(a)(1)(A) and 21 U.S.C. § 881(a)(6). The parties agreed to defer litigation of the forfeiture action during the criminal prosecution. More than a year after the conclusion of the criminal trial, the District Court granted the Government's motion for summary judgment in the civil forfeiture proceeding. Arlt and Wren appealed the decision in the forfeiture action, and the U.S. Court of Appeals reversed, holding that the forfeiture violated the Double Jeopardy Clause.

The U.S. Supreme Court granted certiorari and consolidated both cases.

Held: The Double Jeopardy Clause of the U.S. Constitution does not prevent the Government from punishing defendants for criminal offenses and requiring the forfeiture of their property for the same offenses in separate civil proceedings.

Opinion: Chief Justice REHNQUIST delivered the opinion of the Court.

. . .

I

. . .

II

The Double Jeopardy Clause provides: "[N]or shall any person be subject for the same offence to be twice put in jeopardy of life or limb." The Clause serves the function of preventing both "successive punishments and . . . successive prosecutions." The protection against multiple punishments prohibits the Government from "'punishing twice, or attempting a second time to punish criminally for the same offense.'"

In the decisions that we review, the Courts of Appeals held that the civil forfeitures constituted "punishment," making them subject to the prohibitions of the Double Jeopardy Clause. The Government challenges that characterization of the forfeitures, arguing that the courts were wrong to conclude that civil forfeitures are punitive for double jeopardy purposes.

A

Since the earliest years of this Nation, Congress has authorized the Government to seek parallel in rem civil forfeiture actions and criminal prosecutions based upon the same underlying events. And, in a long line of cases, this Court has considered the application of the Double Jeopardy Clause to civil forfeitures, consistently concluding that the Clause does not apply to such actions because they do not impose punishment.

. . .

B

Our cases reviewing civil forfeitures under the Double Jeopardy Clause adhere to a remarkably consistent theme. . . . [T]he conclusion was the same in each case: in rem civil forfeiture is a remedial civil sanction, distinct from potentially punitive in personam civil penalties such as fines, and does not constitute a punishment under the Double Jeopardy Clause. In the case that we currently review, the Court of Appeals for the Ninth Circuit recognized as much, concluding that . . . "the law was clear that civil forfeitures did not constitute 'punishment' for double jeopardy purposes". . . .

. . .

. . . While a "civil action to recover . . . penalties, is punitive in character," and much like a criminal prosecution in that "it is the wrongdoer in person who is proceeded against . . . and punished," in an in rem forfeiture proceeding, "it is the property which is proceeded against, and by resort to a legal fiction, held guilty and condemned.". . .

. . . Civil penalties are designed as a rough form of "liquidated damages" for the harms suffered by the Government as a result of a defendant's conduct. . . . Whether a "fixed-penalty provision" that seeks to compensate the Government for harm it has suffered is "so extreme" and "so divorced" from the penalty's nonpunitive purpose of compensating the Government as to be a punishment may be determined by balancing the Government's harm against the size of the penalty. Civil forfeitures, in contrast to civil penalties, are designed to do more than simply compensate the Government. Forfeitures serve a variety of purposes, but are designed primarily to confiscate property used in violation of the law, and to require disgorgement of the fruits of illegal conduct. . . .

. . .

C

We turn now to consider the forfeitures in these cases. . . . Because it provides a useful analytical tool, we conduct our inquiry within the framework of the two-part test used in *89 Firearms*.[27] First, we ask whether Congress intended proceedings under 21 U.S.C. § 881, and 18 U.S.C. § 981, to be criminal or civil. Second, we turn to consider whether the proceedings are so punitive in fact as to "persuade us that the forfeiture proceeding[s] may not legitimately be viewed as civil in nature," despite Congress' intent.

There is little doubt that Congress intended these forfeitures to be civil proceedings. . . . "Congress' intent in this regard is most clearly demonstrated by the procedural mechanisms it established for enforcing forfeitures under the statute[s]." . . .

Moving to the second stage of our analysis, we find that there is little evidence, much less the "'clearest proof'" that we require suggesting that forfeiture proceedings under 21 U.S.C. §§ 881(a)(6) and (a)(7), and 18 U.S.C. § 981(a)(1)(A), are so punitive in form and effect as to render them criminal despite Congress' intent to the contrary. The statutes involved in this case are, in most significant respects, indistinguishable from those reviewed, and held not to be punitive, in *Various Items*,[28] *Emerald Cut Stones*,[29] and *89 Firearms*.

Most significant is that § 981(a)(1)(A), and §§ 881(a)(6) and (a)(7), while perhaps having certain punitive aspects, serve important nonpunitive goals. Title 21 U.S.C. § 881(a)(7), under which Ursery's property was forfeited, provides for the forfeiture of "all real property . . . which is used or intended to be used, in any manner or part, to commit, or to facilitate the commission of" a federal drug felony. Requiring the forfeiture of property used to commit federal narcotics violations encourages property owners to take care in managing their property and ensures that they will not permit that property to be used for illegal purposes. In many circumstances, the forfeiture may abate a nuisance.

The forfeiture of the property claimed by Arlt and Wren took place pursuant to 18 U.S.C. § 981(a)(1)(A), and 21 U.S.C. § 881(a)(6). Section 981(a)(1)(A) provides for the forfeiture of "any property" involved in illegal money-laundering transactions. Section 881(a)(6) provides for the forfeiture of "[a]ll . . . things of value furnished or intended to be furnished by any person in exchange for" illegal drugs; "all proceeds traceable to such an exchange"; and "all moneys, negotiable instruments, and securities used or intended to be used to facilitate" a federal drug felony. The same remedial purposes served by § 881(a)(7) are served by § 881(a)(6) and § 981(a)(1)(A). Only one point merits separate discussion. To the extent that § 881(a)(6) applies to "proceeds" of illegal drug activity, it serves the additional nonpunitive goal of ensuring that persons do not profit from their illegal acts.

. . .

We hold that these in rem civil forfeitures are neither "punishment" nor criminal for purposes of the Double Jeopardy Clause. The judgments of the Court of Appeals for the Sixth

---

[27] United States v. One Assortment of 89 Firearms, 465 U.S. 354 (1984).

[28] Various Items of Personal Property v. United States, 282 U.S. 577 (1931).

[29] One Lot of Emerald Cut Stones and One Ring v. United States, 409 U.S. 232 (1972).

Circuit, in No. 95-345, and of the Court of Appeals for the Ninth Circuit, in No. 95-345, are accordingly reversed.

It is so ordered.

Dissent: Justice STEVENS, concurring in the judgment in part and dissenting in part.

The question the Court poses is whether civil forfeitures constitute "punishment" for purposes of the Double Jeopardy Clause. Because the numerous federal statutes authorizing forfeitures cover such a wide variety of situations, it is quite wrong to assume that there is only one answer to that question. For purposes of analysis it is useful to identify three different categories of property that are subject to seizure: proceeds, contraband, and property that has played a part in the commission of a crime. The facts of these two cases illustrate the point.

In No. 95-346 the Government has forfeited $405,089.23 in currency. Those funds are the proceeds of unlawful activity. They are not property that respondents have any right to retain. The forfeiture of such proceeds, like the confiscation of money stolen from a bank, does not punish respondents because it exacts no price in liberty or lawfully derived property from them. I agree that the forfeiture of such proceeds is not punitive and therefore I concur in the Court's disposition of No. 95-346.

None of the property seized in No. 95-345 constituted proceeds of illegal activity. Indeed, the facts of that case reveal a dramatically different situation. Respondent Ursery cultivated marijuana in a heavily wooded area not far from his home in Shiawassee County, Michigan. The illegal substance was consumed by members of his family, but there is no evidence, and no contention by the Government, that he sold any of it to third parties. Acting on the basis of the incorrect assumption that the marijuana plants were on respondent's property, Michigan police officers executed a warrant to search the premises. In his house they found marijuana seeds, stems, stalks, and a growlight. I presume those items were seized, and I have no difficulty concluding that such a seizure does not constitute punishment because respondent had no right to possess contraband. Accordingly, I agree with the Court's opinion insofar as it explains why the forfeiture of contraband does not constitute punishment for double jeopardy purposes.

The critical question presented in No. 95-345 arose, not out of the seizure of contraband by the Michigan police, but rather out of the decision by the United States Attorney to take respondent's home. There is no evidence that the house had been purchased with the proceeds of unlawful activity and the house itself was surely not contraband. Nonetheless, 21 U.S.C. § 881(a)(7) authorized the Government to seek forfeiture of respondent's residence because it had been used to facilitate the manufacture and distribution of marijuana. Respondent was then himself prosecuted for and convicted of manufacturing marijuana. In my opinion none of the reasons supporting the forfeiture of proceeds or contraband provides a sufficient basis for concluding that the confiscation of respondent's home was not punitive.

. . .

Accordingly, I respectfully dissent from the judgment in No. 95-345.

UNITED STATES V. VIRGINIA

SUPREME COURT OF THE UNITED STATES

116 S. Ct. 2264

Decided June 26, 1996

"A purpose genuinely to advance an array of educational options . . . is not served by VMI's historic and constant plan—a plan to 'affor[d] a unique educational benefit only to males.' However 'liberally' this plan serves the State's sons, it makes no provision whatever for her daughters. That is not equal protection."

Background: Since its inception in 1839, the Virginia Military Institute (VMI), a public institution whose mission is to produce "citizen-soldiers," prohibited women from enrolling in its program. In 1990, prompted by a complaint filed with the U.S. Attorney General by a female high-school student seeking admission to VMI, the United States sued the state of Virginia and VMI, alleging that VMI's exclusively male admission policy violated the Fourteenth Amendment's Equal Protection Clause by discriminating against women without persuasive justification. The Federal District Court held that VMI's admission policy was constitutional. The U.S. Court of Appeals reversed and held that VMI's admission policy violated the Equal Protection Clause of the Constitution. In response, Virginia proposed a parallel program for women—the Virginia Women's Institute for Leadership (VWIL)—which would be located at Mary Baldwin College, a private liberal arts school for women. The District Court held that Virginia's proposal made VMI's exclusively male admission policy constitutional. The Court of Appeals upheld the District Court's decision. The United States appealed.

Held: Virginia's categorical exclusion of women from the unique educational opportunities provided by VMI denied equal protection to women.

Opinion: Justice GINSBURG delivered the opinion of the Court.

I

. . .

II

. . .

III

The cross-petitions in this case present two ultimate issues. First, does Virginia's exclusion of women from the educational opportunities provided by VMI—extraordinary opportunities for military training and civilian leadership development—deny to women "capable of all of the individual activities required of VMI cadets," the equal protection of the laws guaranteed by the Fourteenth Amendment? Second, if VMI's "unique" situation—as Virginia's

91

sole single-sex public institution of higher education—offends the Constitution's equal protection principle, what is the remedial requirement?

IV

. . .

. . . To summarize the Court's current directions for cases of official classification based on gender: Focusing on the differential treatment or denial of opportunity for which relief is sought, the reviewing court must determine whether the proffered justification is "exceedingly persuasive." The burden of justification is demanding and it rests entirely on the State. The State must show "at least that the [challenged] classification serves 'important governmental objectives and that the discriminatory means employed' are 'substantially related to the achievement of those objectives.'" The justification must be genuine, not hypothesized or invented post hoc in response to litigation. And it must not rely on overbroad generalizations about the different talents, capacities, or preferences of males and females.

The heightened review standard our precedent establishes does not make sex a proscribed classification. Supposed "inherent differences" are no longer accepted as a ground for race or national origin classifications. Physical differences between men and women, however, are enduring: "[T]he two sexes are not fungible; a community made up exclusively of one [sex] is different from a community composed of both."

"Inherent differences" between men and women, we have come to appreciate, remain cause for celebration, but not for denigration of the members of either sex or for artificial constraints on an individual's opportunity. Sex classifications may be used to compensate women "for particular economic disabilities [they have] suffered" to advance full development of the talent and capacities of our Nation's people. But such classifications may not be used, as they once were to create or perpetuate the legal, social, and economic inferiority of women.

Measuring the record in this case against the review standard just described, we conclude that Virginia has shown no "exceedingly persuasive justification" for excluding all women from the citizen-soldier training afforded by VMI. We therefore affirm the Fourth Circuit's initial judgment, which held that Virginia had violated the Fourteenth Amendment's Equal Protection Clause. Because the remedy proffered by Virginia—the Mary Baldwin VWIL program—does not cure the constitutional violation, i.e., it does not provide equal opportunity, we reverse the Fourth Circuit's final judgment in this case.

V

. . . Virginia . . . asserts two justifications in defense of VMI's exclusion of women. First, the Commonwealth contends, "single-sex education provides important educational benefits," and the option of single-sex education contributes to "diversity in educational approaches." Second, the Commonwealth argues, "the unique VMI method of character development and leadership training," the school's adversative approach, would have to be modified were VMI to admit women. We consider these two justifications in turn.

A

Single-sex education affords pedagogical benefits to at least some students, Virginia emphasizes, and that reality is uncontested in this litigation. Similarly, it is not disputed that diversity among public educational institutions can serve the public good. But Virginia has not shown that VMI was established, or has been maintained, with a view to diversifying, by its

UNITED STATES V. GUY JEROME URSERY

UNITED STATES V. $405,089.23 IN UNITED STATES CURRENCY

Supreme Court of the United States

116 S. Ct. 2135

Decided June 24, 1996

"It is well settled that 'Congress may impose both a criminal and a civil sanction in respect to the same act or omission.' By itself, the fact that a forfeiture statute has some connection to a criminal violation is far from the 'clearest proof' necessary to show that a proceeding is criminal."

Background: In Case No. 95-345, Michigan police found marijuana growing adjacent to Guy Ursery's house, and discovered marijuana seeds, stems, stalks, and a growlight within the house. The United States instituted civil forfeiture proceedings against the house, alleging that the property was subject to forfeiture under a federal law (21 U.S.C. § 881(a)(7)) because it had been used for several years to facilitate the unlawful processing and distribution of a controlled substance. Ursery ultimately paid the United States $13,250 to settle the forfeiture claim in full. Shortly before the settlement was consummated, Ursery was criminally indicted for manufacturing marijuana, in violation of Section 841(a)(1) of 21 U.S.C. A jury found him guilty. The U.S. Court of Appeals reversed Ursery's criminal conviction, holding that the conviction violated the Double Jeopardy Clause of the United States Constitution.

In Case No. 95-346, Charles Wesley Arlt and James Wren were convicted of conspiracy to aid and abet the manufacture of methamphetamine, conspiracy to launder monetary instruments, and numerous counts of money laundering. Before the criminal trial had started, the United States had filed an in rem civil complaint (that is, an impersonal proceeding against property) against various items of property seized from, or titled to, Arlt and Wren, or Payback Mines, a corporation controlled by Arlt. The complaint alleged that each piece of property was subject to forfeiture under both 18 U.S.C. § 981(a)(1)(A) and 21 U.S.C. § 881(a)(6). The parties agreed to defer litigation of the forfeiture action during the criminal prosecution. More than a year after the conclusion of the criminal trial, the District Court granted the Government's motion for summary judgment in the civil forfeiture proceeding. Arlt and Wren appealed the decision in the forfeiture action, and the U.S. Court of Appeals reversed, holding that the forfeiture violated the Double Jeopardy Clause.

The U.S. Supreme Court granted certiorari and consolidated both cases.

Held: The Double Jeopardy Clause of the U.S. Constitution does not prevent the Government from punishing defendants for criminal offenses and requiring the forfeiture of their property for the same offenses in separate civil proceedings.

Opinion: Chief Justice REHNQUIST delivered the opinion of the Court.

. . .

I

. . .

II

The Double Jeopardy Clause provides: "[N]or shall any person be subject for the same offence to be twice put in jeopardy of life or limb." The Clause serves the function of preventing both "successive punishments and . . . successive prosecutions." The protection against multiple punishments prohibits the Government from "'punishing twice, or attempting a second time to punish criminally for the same offense.'"

In the decisions that we review, the Courts of Appeals held that the civil forfeitures constituted "punishment," making them subject to the prohibitions of the Double Jeopardy Clause. The Government challenges that characterization of the forfeitures, arguing that the courts were wrong to conclude that civil forfeitures are punitive for double jeopardy purposes.

A

Since the earliest years of this Nation, Congress has authorized the Government to seek parallel in rem civil forfeiture actions and criminal prosecutions based upon the same underlying events. And, in a long line of cases, this Court has considered the application of the Double Jeopardy Clause to civil forfeitures, consistently concluding that the Clause does not apply to such actions because they do not impose punishment.

. . .

B

Our cases reviewing civil forfeitures under the Double Jeopardy Clause adhere to a remarkably consistent theme. . . . [T]he conclusion was the same in each case: in rem civil forfeiture is a remedial civil sanction, distinct from potentially punitive in personam civil penalties such as fines, and does not constitute a punishment under the Double Jeopardy Clause. In the case that we currently review, the Court of Appeals for the Ninth Circuit recognized as much, concluding that . . . "the law was clear that civil forfeitures did not constitute 'punishment' for double jeopardy purposes". . . .

. . .

. . . While a "civil action to recover . . . penalties, is punitive in character," and much like a criminal prosecution in that "it is the wrongdoer in person who is proceeded against . . . and punished," in an in rem forfeiture proceeding, "it is the property which is proceeded against, and by resort to a legal fiction, held guilty and condemned.". . .

. . . Civil penalties are designed as a rough form of "liquidated damages" for the harms suffered by the Government as a result of a defendant's conduct. . . . Whether a "fixed-penalty provision" that seeks to compensate the Government for harm it has suffered is "so extreme" and "so divorced" from the penalty's nonpunitive purpose of compensating the Government as to be a punishment may be determined by balancing the Government's harm against the size of the penalty. Civil forfeitures, in contrast to civil penalties, are designed to do more than simply compensate the Government. Forfeitures serve a variety of purposes, but are designed primarily categorical exclusion of women, educational opportunities within the State. In cases of this genre, our precedent instructs that "benign" justifications proffered in defense of categorical exclusions will not be accepted automatically; a tenable justification must describe actual state purposes, not rationalizations for actions in fact differently grounded.

. . .

. . . In 1839, when the State established VMI, a range of educational opportunities for men and women was scarcely contemplated. Higher education at the time was considered dangerous for women; reflecting widely held views about women's proper place, the Nation's first universities and colleges—for example, Harvard in Massachusetts, William and Mary in Virginia—admitted only men. . . .

. . .

. . . A purpose genuinely to advance an array of educational options, as the Court of Appeals recognized, is not served by VMI's historic and constant plan—a plan to "affor[d] a unique educational benefit only to males." However "liberally" this plan serves the State's sons, it makes no provision whatever for her daughters. That is not equal protection.

B

Virginia next argues that VMI's adversative method of training provides educational benefits that cannot be made available, unmodified, to women. Alterations to accommodate women would necessarily be "radical," so "drastic," Virginia asserts, as to transform, indeed "destroy," VMI's program. Neither sex would be favored by the transformation, Virginia maintains: Men would be deprived of the unique opportunity currently available to them; women would not gain that opportunity because their participation would "eliminat[e] the very aspects of [the] program that distinguish [VMI] from . . . other institutions of higher education in Virginia."

. . . [I]t is uncontested that women's admission would require accommodations, primarily in arranging housing assignments and physical training programs for female cadets. It is also undisputed, however, that "the VMI methodology could be used to educate women". . . .

. . .

The notion that admission of women would downgrade VMI's stature, destroy the adversative system and, with it, even the school, is a judgment hardly proved, a prediction hardly different from other "self-fulfilling prophec[ies]," once routinely used to deny rights or opportunities. . . .

. . .

Women's successful entry into the federal military academies, and their participation in the Nation's military forces, indicate that Virginia's fears for the future of VMI may not be solidly grounded. The State's justification for excluding all women from "citizen-soldier" training for which some are qualified, in any event, cannot rank as "exceedingly persuasive," as we have explained and applied that standard.

. . .

VI

In the second phase of the litigation, Virginia presented its remedial plan—maintain VMI as a male-only college and create VWIL as a separate program for women. . . .

A

A remedial decree, this Court has said, must closely fit the constitutional violation; it must be shaped to place persons unconstitutionally denied an opportunity or advantage in "the position they would have occupied in the absence of [discrimination]." The constitutional violation in this case is the categorical exclusion of women from an extraordinary educational opportunity afforded men. A proper remedy for an unconstitutional exclusion, we have explained, aims to "eliminate [so far as possible] the discriminatory effects of the past" and to "bar like discrimination in the future."

Virginia chose not to eliminate, but to leave untouched, VMI's exclusionary policy. For women only, however, Virginia proposed a separate program, different in kind from VMI and unequal in tangible and intangible facilities. Having violated the Constitution's equal protection requirement, Virginia was obliged to show that its remedial proposal "directly address[ed] and relate[d] to" the violation, i.e., the equal protection denied to women ready, willing, and able to benefit from educational opportunities of the kind VMI offers. Virginia described VWIL as a "parallel program," and asserted that VWIL shares VMI's mission of producing "citizen-soldiers" and VMI's goals of providing "education, military training, mental and physical discipline, character . . . and leadership development." If the VWIL program could not "eliminate the discriminatory effects of the past," could it at least "bar like discrimination in the future?" A comparison of the programs said to be "parallel" informs our answer. In exposing the character of, and differences in, the VMI and VWIL programs, we recapitulate facts earlier presented.

VWIL affords women no opportunity to experience the rigorous military training for which VMI is famed. Instead, the VWIL program "deemphasize[s]" military education and uses a "cooperative method" of education "which reinforces self-esteem."

VWIL students participate in ROTC and a "largely ceremonial" Virginia Corps of Cadets, but Virginia deliberately did not make VWIL a military Institute. The VWIL House is not a military-style residence and VWIL students need not live together throughout the 4-year program, eat meals together, or wear uniforms during the school day. VWIL students thus do not experience the "barracks" life "crucial to the VMI experience," the Spartan living arrangements designed to foster an "egalitarian ethic". . . .

. . . Kept away from the pressures, hazards, and psychological bonding characteristic of VMI's adversative training, VWIL students will not know the "feeling of tremendous accomplishment" commonly experienced by VMI's successful cadets.

Virginia maintains that these methodological differences are "justified pedagogically," based on "important differences between men and women in learning and developmental needs," "psychological and sociological differences" Virginia describes as "real" and "not stereotypes". . . .

As earlier stated, generalizations about "the way women are," estimates of what is appropriate for most women, no longer justify denying opportunity to women whose talent and capacity place them outside the average description. Notably, Virginia never asserted that VMI's method of education suits most men. It is also revealing that Virginia accounted for its failure to make the VWIL experience "the entirely militaristic experience of VMI" on the ground that VWIL "is planned for women who do not necessarily expect to pursue military careers." By that reasoning, VMI's "entirely militaristic" program would be inappropriate for men in general or as a group, for "[o]nly about 15% of VMI cadets enter career military service."

In contrast to the generalizations about women on which Virginia rests, we note again these dispositive realities: VMI's "implementing methodology" is not "inherently unsuitable to women"; "some women . . . do well under [the] adversative model"; "some women, at least, would want to attend [VMI] if they had the opportunity"; "some women are capable of all of the individual activities required of VMI cadets"; and "can meet the physical standards [VMI] now impose[s] on men." It is on behalf of these women that the United States has instituted this suit, and it is for them that a remedy must be crafted, a remedy that will end their exclusion from a state-supplied educational opportunity for which they are fit, a decree that will "bar like discrimination in the future."

B

In myriad respects other than military training, VWIL does not qualify as VMI's equal. VWIL's student body, faculty, course offerings, and facilities hardly match VMI's. Nor can the VWIL graduate anticipate the benefits associated with VMI's 157-year history, the school's prestige, and its influential alumni network .

. . .

. . . [W]e rule here that Virginia has not shown substantial equality in the separate educational opportunities the State supports at VWIL and VMI.

C

. . .

VII

. . .

VMI . . . offers an educational opportunity no other Virginia institution provides, and the school's "prestige"—associated with its success in developing "citizen-soldiers"—is unequaled. Virginia has closed this facility to its daughters and, instead, has devised for them a "parallel program," with a faculty less impressively credentialed and less well paid, more limited course offerings, fewer opportunities for military training and for scientific specialization. VMI, beyond question, "possesses to a far greater degree" than the VWIL program "those qualities which are incapable of objective measurement but which make for greatness in a . . . school," including "position and influence of the alumni, standing in the community, traditions and prestige." Women seeking and fit for a VMI-quality education cannot be offered anything less, under the State's obligation to afford them genuinely equal protection.

. . .

* * *

For the reasons stated, the initial judgment of the Court of Appeals is affirmed, the final judgment of the Court of Appeals is reversed, and the case is remanded for further proceedings consistent with this opinion.

It is so ordered.

Dissent: Justice SCALIA, dissenting.

. . . [The Court] rejects (contrary to our established practice) the factual findings of two courts below, sweeps aside the precedents of this Court, and ignores the history of our people. As to facts: it explicitly rejects the finding that there exist "gender-based developmental differences" supporting Virginia's restriction of the "adversative" method to only a men's institution, and the finding that the all-male composition of the Virginia Military Institute (VMI) is essential to that institution's character. As to precedent: it drastically revises our established standards for reviewing sex-based classifications. And as to history: it counts for nothing the long tradition, enduring down to the present, of men's military colleges supported by both States and the Federal Government.

. . .

I

. . .

. . . [I]n my view the function of this Court is to preserve our society's values regarding (among other things) equal protection, not to revise them; to prevent backsliding from the degree of restriction the Constitution imposed upon democratic government, not to prescribe, on our own authority, progressively higher degrees. For that reason it is my view that, whatever abstract tests we may choose to devise, they cannot supersede—and indeed ought to be crafted so as to reflect—those constant and unbroken national traditions that embody the people's understanding of ambiguous constitutional texts. More specifically, it is my view that "when a practice not expressly prohibited by the text of the Bill of Rights bears the endorsement of a long tradition of open, widespread, and unchallenged use that dates back to the beginning of the Republic, we have no proper basis for striking it down". . . .

The all-male constitution of VMI comes squarely within such a governing tradition. Founded by the Commonwealth of Virginia in 1839 and continuously maintained by it since, VMI has always admitted only men. And in that regard it has not been unusual. For almost all of VMI's more than a century and a half of existence, its single-sex status reflected the uniform practice for government-supported military colleges. Another famous Southern institution, The Citadel, has existed as a state-funded school of South Carolina since 1842. And all the federal military colleges—West Point, the Naval Academy at Annapolis, and even the Air Force Academy, which was not established until 1954—admitted only males for most of their history. Their admission of women in 1976 (upon which the Court today relies), came not by court decree, but because the people, through their elected representatives, decreed a change. In other words, the tradition of having government-funded military schools for men is as well rooted in the traditions of this country as the tradition of sending only men into military combat. The people may decide to change the one tradition, like the other, through democratic processes; but the assertion that either tradition has been unconstitutional through the centuries is not law, but politics-smuggled-into-law.

. . .

Today, however, change is forced upon Virginia, and reversion to single-sex education is prohibited nationwide, not by democratic processes but by order of this Court. Even while bemoaning the sorry, bygone days of "fixed notions" concerning women's education, the Court favors current notions so fixedly that it is willing to write them into the Constitution of the United States by application of custom-built "tests." This is not the interpretation of a Constitution, but the creation of one.

II

To reject the Court's disposition today, however, it is not necessary to accept my view that the Court's made-up tests cannot displace longstanding national traditions as the primary determinant of what the Constitution means. It is only necessary to apply honestly the test the Court has been applying to sex-based classifications for the past two decades. It is well settled, as Justice O'CONNOR stated some time ago for a unanimous Court, that we evaluate a statutory classification based on sex under a standard that lies "[b]etween th[e] extremes of rational basis review and strict scrutiny." We have denominated this standard "intermediate scrutiny" and under it have inquired whether the statutory classification is "substantially related to an important governmental objective."

. . .

Although the Court in two places . . . asks whether the State has demonstrated "that the classification serves important governmental objectives and that the discriminatory means employed are substantially related to the achievement of those objectives," the Court never answers the question presented in anything resembling that form. When it engages in analysis, the Court instead prefers the phrase "exceedingly persuasive justification". . . .

. . .

Only the amorphous "exceedingly persuasive justification" phrase, and not the standard elaboration of intermediate scrutiny, can be made to yield this conclusion that VMI's single-sex composition is unconstitutional because there exist several women (or, one would have to conclude under the Court's reasoning, a single woman) willing and able to undertake VMI's program. . . .

. . .

III

With this explanation of how the Court has succeeded in making its analysis seem orthodox—and indeed, if intimations are to be believed, even overly generous to VMI—I now proceed to describe how the analysis should have been conducted. The question to be answered, I repeat, is whether the exclusion of women from VMI is "substantially related to an important governmental objective."

A

It is beyond question that Virginia has an important state interest in providing effective college education for its citizens. That single-sex instruction is an approach substantially related to that interest should be evident enough from the long and continuing history in this country of men's and women's colleges. . . .

. . .

B

The Court today has no adequate response to this clear demonstration of the conclusion produced by application of intermediate scrutiny. Rather, it relies on a series of contentions that are irrelevant or erroneous as a matter of law, foreclosed by the record in this case, or both.

. . .

C

. . .

IV

As is frequently true, the Court's decision today will have consequences that extend far beyond the parties to the case. What I take to be the Court's unease with these consequences, and its resulting unwillingness to acknowledge them, cannot alter the reality.

A

Under the constitutional principles announced and applied today, single-sex public education is unconstitutional. By going through the motions of applying a balancing test—asking whether the State has adduced an "exceedingly persuasive justification" for its sex-based classification—the Court creates the illusion that government officials in some future case will have a clear shot at justifying some sort of single-sex public education. Indeed, the Court seeks to create even a greater illusion than that: It purports to have said nothing of relevance to other public schools at all. "We address specifically and only an educational opportunity recognized . . . as 'unique'". . . .

The Supreme Court of the United States does not sit to announce "unique" dispositions. Its principal function is to establish precedent—that is, to set forth principles of law that every court in America must follow. As we said only this Term, we expect both ourselves and lower courts to adhere to the "rationale upon which the Court based the results of its earlier decisions." That is the principal reason we publish our opinions.

And the rationale of today's decision is sweeping: for sex-based classifications, a redefinition of intermediate scrutiny that makes it indistinguishable from strict scrutiny. Indeed, the Court indicates that if any program restricted to one sex is "uniqu[e]," it must be opened to members of the opposite sex "who have the will and capacity" to participate in it. I suggest that the single-sex program that will not be capable of being characterized as "unique" is not only unique but nonexistent.

In any event, regardless of whether the Court's rationale leaves some small amount of room for lawyers to argue, it ensures that single-sex public education is functionally dead. The costs of litigating the constitutionality of a single-sex education program, and the risks of ultimately losing that litigation, are simply too high to be embraced by public officials. Any person with standing to challenge any sex-based classification can haul the State into federal court and compel it to establish by evidence (presumably in the form of expert testimony) that there is an "exceedingly persuasive justification" for the classification. Should the courts happen to interpret that vacuous phrase as establishing a standard that is not utterly impossible of achievement, there is considerable risk that whether the standard has been met will not be determined on the basis of the record evidence—indeed, that will necessarily be the approach of any court that seeks to walk the path the Court has trod today. No state official in his right mind will buy such a high-cost, high-risk lawsuit by commencing a single-sex program. The enemies of single-sex education have won; by persuading only seven Justices (five would have been enough) that their view of the world is enshrined in the Constitution, they have effectively imposed that view on all 50 States.

. . .

B

There are few extant single-sex public educational programs. The potential of today's decision for widespread disruption of existing institutions lies in its application to private single-sex education. Government support is immensely important to private educational institutions. . . .

. . .

The only hope for state-assisted single-sex private schools is that the Court will not apply in the future the principles of law it has applied today. That is a substantial hope, I am happy and ashamed to say. After all, did not the Court today abandon the principles of law it has applied in our earlier sex-classification cases? And does not the Court positively invite private colleges to rely upon our ad-hocery by assuring them this case is "unique"? I would not advise the foundation of any new single-sex college (especially an all-male one) with the expectation of being allowed to receive any government support; but it is too soon to abandon in despair those single-sex colleges already in existence. It will certainly be possible for this Court to write a future opinion that ignores the broad principles of law set forth today, and that characterizes as utterly dispositive the opinion's perceptions that VMI was a uniquely prestigious all-male institution, conceived in chauvinism, etc., etc. I will not join that opinion.

. . .

UNITED STATES V. WINSTAR CORPORATION

SUPREME COURT OF THE UNITED STATES

116 S. Ct. 2432

Decided July 1, 1996

"It would, indeed, have been madness for respondents to have engaged in these transactions with no more protection than the Government's reading would have given them, for the very existence of their institutions would then have been in jeopardy from the moment their agreements were signed."

Background: Realizing that the Federal Savings and Loan Insurance Corporation (FSLIC) lacked the funds to liquidate all of the failing thrifts during the savings and loan crisis of the 1980s, the Federal Home Loan Bank Board (Bank Board) encouraged healthy thrifts and outside investors to take over ailing thrifts in a series of "supervisory mergers." As an inducement, the Bank Board agreed to permit the acquiring entities to designate the excess of the purchase price over the fair value of identifiable assets as an intangible asset referred to as supervisory goodwill, and to count such goodwill and certain capital credits toward the capital reserve requirements imposed by federal regulations. Congress subsequently passed of the Financial Institutions Reform, Recovery, and Enforcement Act of 1989 (FIRREA), which prohibited thrifts from counting goodwill and capital credits in computing the required reserves. Two thrifts created by way of supervisory mergers were seized and liquidated by federal regulators for failure to meet FIRREA's capital requirements, and a third avoided seizure through a private recapitalization.

Believing that the Bank Board and FSLIC had promised that they could count supervisory goodwill toward regulatory capital requirements, the three thrifts each filed suit against the United States in the Court of Federal Claims, seeking damages for breach of contract. In granting each thrift's motion for summary judgment, the court held that the Government had breached its contractual obligations. The cases were consolidated, and the en banc U.S. Court of Appeals for the Federal Circuit affirmed. The United States appealed.

Held: The United States breached contracts to permit financial institutions to use special accounting methods with regard to their acquisitions of failing thrifts when its agencies, pursuant to FIRREA, barred use of those methods.

Opinion: Justice SOUTER announced the judgment of the Court and delivered an opinion, in which Justice STEVENS and Justice BREYER join, and in which Justice O'CONNOR joins except as to Parts IV-A and IV-B.

The issue in this case is the enforceability of contracts between the Government and participants in a regulated industry, to accord them particular regulatory treatment in exchange for their assumption of liabilities that threatened to produce claims against the Government as

101

insurer.   Although Congress subsequently changed the relevant law, and thereby barred the Government from specifically honoring its agreements, we hold that the terms assigning the risk of regulatory change to the Government are enforceable, and that the Government is therefore liable in damages for breach.

I

. . .

II

We took this case to consider the extent to which special rules, not generally applicable to private contracts, govern enforcement of the governmental contracts at issue here. We decide whether the Government may assert four special defenses to respondents' claims for breach: the canon of contract construction that surrenders of sovereign authority must appear in unmistakable terms, *Bowen v. Public Agencies Opposed to Social Security Entrapment*;[30] the rule that an agent's authority to make such surrenders must be delegated in express terms, *Home Telephone & Telegraph Co. v. City of Los Angeles*;[31] the doctrine that a government may not, in any event, contract to surrender certain reserved powers, *Stone v. Mississippi*;[32] and, finally, the principle that a Government's sovereign acts do not give rise to a claim for breach of contract, *Horowitz v. United States*.[33]

. . .

A

The Federal Circuit found that "[t]he three plaintiff thrifts negotiated contracts with the bank regulatory agencies that allowed them to include supervisory goodwill (and capital credits) as assets for regulatory capital purposes and to amortize that supervisory goodwill over extended periods of time." Although each of these transactions was fundamentally similar, the relevant circumstances and documents vary somewhat from case to case.

1

. . .

2

. . .

3

. . .

B

It is important to be clear about what these contracts did and did not require of the Government. Nothing in the documentation or the circumstances of these transactions purported to bar the Government from changing the way in which it regulated the thrift industry. Rather, . . . "the Bank Board and the FSLIC were contractually bound to recognize the supervisory goodwill and the amortization periods reflected" in the agreements between the parties. We read this promise as the law of contracts has always treated promises to provide something beyond the promisor's absolute control, that is, as a promise to insure the promisee against loss arising from the promised condition's nonoccurrence. . . .

---

[30] 477 U.S. 41 (1986).
[31] 211 U.S. 265 (1908).
[32] 101 U.S. 814 (1880).
[33] 267 U.S. 458 (1925).

When the law as to capital requirements changed in the present instance, the Government was unable to perform its promise and, therefore, became liable for breach. We accept the Federal Circuit's conclusion that the Government breached these contracts when, pursuant to the new regulatory capital requirements imposed by FIRREA, 12 U.S.C. § 1464(t), the federal regulatory agencies limited the use of supervisory goodwill and capital credits in calculating respondents' net worth. In the case of Winstar and Statesman, the Government exacerbated its breach when it seized and liquidated respondents' thrifts for regulatory noncompliance.

. . .

III

The Government argues for reversal, first, on the principle that "contracts that limit the government's future exercises of regulatory authority are strongly disfavored; such contracts will be recognized only rarely, and then only when the limitation on future regulatory authority is expressed in unmistakable terms." Hence, the Government says, the agreements between the Bank Board, FSLIC, and respondents should not be construed to waive Congress's authority to enact a subsequent bar to using supervisory goodwill and capital credits to meet regulatory capital requirements.

The argument mistakes the scope of the unmistakability doctrine. The thrifts do not claim that the Bank Board and FSLIC purported to bind Congress to ossify the law in conformity to the contracts; they seek no injunction against application of FIRREA's new capital requirements to them and no exemption from FIRREA's terms. They simply claim that the Government assumed the risk that subsequent changes in the law might prevent it from performing, and agreed to pay damages in the event that such failure to perform caused financial injury. The question, then, is not whether Congress could be constrained but whether the doctrine of unmistakability is applicable to any contract claim against the Government for breach occasioned by a subsequent act of Congress. The answer to this question is no.

A

. . .

B

The answer to the Government's unmistakability argument also meets its two related contentions on the score of ultra vires: that the Bank Board and FSLIC had no authority to bargain away Congress's power to change the law in the future, and that we should in any event find no such authority conferred without an express delegation to that effect. The first of these positions rests on the reserved powers doctrine, developed in the course of litigating claims that States had violated the Contract Clause. It holds that a state government may not contract away "an essential attribute of its sovereignty," with the classic example of its limitation on the scope of the Contract Clause being found in *Stone v. Mississippi*. There a corporation bargained for and received a state legislative charter to conduct lotteries, only to have them outlawed by statute a year later. This Court rejected the argument that the charter immunized the corporation from the operation of the statute, holding that "the legislature cannot bargain away the police power of a State."

The Government says that "[t]he logic of the doctrine . . . applies equally to contracts alleged to have been made by the federal government." This may be so but is also beside the point, for the reason that the Government's ability to set capital requirements is not limited by the Bank Board's and FSLIC's promises to make good any losses arising from subsequent regulatory changes. The answer to the Government's contention that the State cannot barter away certain elements of its sovereign power is that a contract to adjust the risk of subsequent legislative change does not strip the Government of its legislative sovereignty.

The same response answers the Government's demand for express delegation of any purported authority to fetter the exercise of sovereign power. It is true, of course, that in *Home Telephone & Telegraph Co. v. City of Los Angeles*, we said that "[t]he surrender, by contract, of a power of government, though in certain well-defined cases it may be made by legislative authority, is a very grave act, and the surrender itself, as well as the authority to make it, must be closely scrutinized." Hence, where "a contract has the effect of extinguishing pro tanto an undoubted power of government," we have insisted that "both [the contract's] existence and the authority to make it must clearly and unmistakably appear, and all doubts must be resolved in favor of the continuance of the power." But *Home Telephone & Telegraph* simply has no application to the present case, because there were no contracts to surrender the Government's sovereign power to regulate.

There is no question, conversely, that the Bank Board and FSLIC had ample statutory authority to do what the Court of Federal Claims and the Federal Circuit found they did do, that is, promise to permit respondents to count supervisory goodwill and capital credits toward regulatory capital and to pay respondents' damages if that performance became impossible. The organic statute creating FSLIC as an arm of the Bank Board, 12 U.S.C. § 1725(c) (1988 ed.) (repealed 1989), generally empowered it "[t]o make contracts," and § 1729(f)(2), enacted in 1978, delegated more specific powers in the context of supervisory mergers. . . .

Nor is there any reason to suppose that the breadth of this authority was not meant to extend to contracts governing treatment of regulatory capital. Congress specifically recognized FSLIC's authority to permit thrifts to count goodwill toward capital requirements when it modified the National Housing Act in 1987. . . .

IV

The Government's final line of defense is the sovereign acts doctrine, to the effect that "'[w]hatever acts the government may do, be they legislative or executive, so long as they be public and general, cannot be deemed specially to alter, modify, obstruct or violate the particular contracts into which it enters with private persons.'" Because FIRREA's alteration of the regulatory capital requirements was a "public and general act," the Government says, that act could not amount to a breach of the Government's contract with respondents.

The Government's position cannot prevail, however, for two independent reasons. The facts of this case do not warrant application of the doctrine, and even if that were otherwise the doctrine would not suffice to excuse liability under this governmental contract allocating risks of regulatory change in a highly regulated industry.

. . .

The Government argues that "[t]he relevant question [under these cases] is whether the impact [of governmental action] . . . is caused by a law enacted to govern regulatory policy and to advance the general welfare." This understanding assumes that the dual characters of Government as contractor and legislator are never "fused" . . . so long as the object of the statute is regulatory and meant to accomplish some public good. That is, on the Government's reading, a regulatory object is proof against treating the legislature as having acted to avoid the

Government's contractual obligations, in which event the sovereign acts defense would not be applicable. But the Government's position is open to serious objection.

As an initial matter, we have already expressed our doubt that a workable line can be drawn between the Government's "regulatory" and "nonregulatory" capacities. . . .

An even more serious objection is that allowing the Government to avoid contractual liability merely by passing any "regulatory statute," would flaunt the general principle that, "[w]hen the United States enters into contract relations, its rights and duties therein are governed generally by the law applicable to contracts between private individuals." Careful attention to the cases shows that the sovereign acts doctrine was meant to serve this principle, not undermine it. . . .

A

If the Government is to be treated like other contractors, some line has to be drawn in situations like the one before us between regulatory legislation that is relatively free of government self-interest and therefore cognizable for the purpose of a legal impossibility defense and, on the other hand, statutes tainted by a governmental object of self-relief. Such an object is not necessarily inconsistent with a public purpose, of course, and when we speak of governmental "self-interest," we simply mean to identify instances in which the Government seeks to shift the costs of meeting its legitimate public responsibilities to private parties. Hence, while the Government might legitimately conclude that a given contractual commitment was no longer in the public interest, a government seeking relief from such commitments through legislation would obviously not be in a position comparable to that of the private contractor who willy-nilly was barred by law from performance. There would be, then, good reason in such circumstance to find the regulatory and contractual characters of the Government fused together . . . so that the Government should not have the benefit of the defense.

Horowitz's criterion of "public and general act" thus reflects the traditional "rule of law" assumption that generality in the terms by which the use of power is authorized will tend to guard against its misuse to burden or benefit the few unjustifiably. Hence, governmental action will not be held against the Government for purposes of the impossibility defense so long as the action's impact upon public contracts is . . . merely incidental to the accomplishment of a broader governmental objective. The greater the Government's self-interest, however, the more suspect becomes the claim that its private contracting partners ought to bear the financial burden of the Government's own improvidence, and where a substantial part of the impact of the Government's action rendering performance impossible falls on its own contractual obligations, the defense will be unavailable.

. . .

B

In the present case, it is impossible to attribute the exculpatory "public and general" character to FIRREA. Although we have not been told the dollar value of the relief the Government would obtain if insulated from liability under contracts such as these, the attention given to the regulatory contracts prior to passage of FIRREA shows that a substantial effect on governmental contracts is certain. The statute not only had the purpose of eliminating the very accounting gimmicks that acquiring thrifts had been promised, but the specific object of abrogating enough of the acquisition contracts as to make that consequence of the legislation a focal point of the congressional debate. . . . Representative Rostenkowski, for example, insisted that "the Federal Government should be able to change requirements when they have proven to be disastrous and contrary to the public interest. The contracts between the savings and loan owners when they acquired failing institutions in the early 1980's are not contracts written in stone."

This evidence of intense concern with contracts like the ones before us suffices to show that FIRREA had the substantial effect of releasing the Government from its own contractual obligations. Congress obviously expected FIRREA to have such an effect, and in the absence of any evidence to the contrary we accept its factual judgment that this would be so. Nor is Congress's own judgment neutralized by the fact, emphasized by the Government, that FIRREA did not formally target particular transactions. Legislation can almost always be written in a formally general way, and the want of an identified target is not much security when a measure's impact nonetheless falls substantially upon the Government's contracting partners. For like reason, it does not answer the legislative record to insist, as the Government does, that the congressional focus is irrelevant because the broad purpose of FIRREA was to "advance the general welfare." We assume nothing less of all congressional action, with the result that an intent to benefit the public can no more serve as a criterion of a "public and general" sovereign act than its regulatory character can. While our limited enquiry into the background and evolution of the thrift crisis leaves us with the understanding that Congress acted to protect the public in the FIRREA legislation, the extent to which this reform relieved the Government of its own contractual obligations precludes a finding that the statute is a "public and general" act for purposes of the sovereign acts defense.

C

Even if FIRREA were to qualify as "public and general," however, other fundamental reasons would leave the sovereign acts doctrine inadequate to excuse the Government's breach of these contracts. As *Horowitz* makes clear, that defense simply relieves the Government as contractor from the traditional blanket rule that a contracting party may not obtain discharge if its own act rendered performance impossible. But even if the Government stands in the place of a private party with respect to "public and general" sovereign acts, it does not follow that discharge will always be available, for the common-law doctrine of impossibility imposes additional requirements before a party may avoid liability for breach. . . . Thus, since the object of the sovereign acts defense is to place the Government as contractor on par with a private contractor in the same circumstances, the Government, like any other defending party in a contract action, must show that the passage of the statute rendering its performance impossible was an event contrary to the basic assumptions on which the parties agreed, and must ultimately show that the language or circumstances do not indicate that the Government should be liable in any case. While we do not say that these conditions can never be satisfied when the Government contracts with participants in a regulated industry for particular regulatory treatment, we find that the Government as such a contractor has not satisfied the conditions for discharge in the present case.

1

For a successful impossibility defense the Government would have to show that the nonoccurrence of regulatory amendment was a basic assumption of these contracts. The premise of this requirement is that the parties will have bargained with respect to any risks that are both within their contemplation and central to the substance of the contract; as Justice Traynor said, "[i]f [the risk] was foreseeable there should have been provision for it in the contract, and the absence of such a provision gives rise to the inference that the risk was assumed." That inference is particularly compelling, where, as here, the contract provides for particular regulatory treatment (and, a fortiori, allocates the risk of regulatory change). Such an agreement reflects the inescapable recognition that regulated industries in the modern world do not live under the law of the Medes and the Persians, and the very fact that such a contract is made at all is at odds with any assumption of regulatory stasis. In this particular case, whether or not the reach of the FIRREA reforms was anticipated by the parties, there is no doubt that some changes in the regulatory structure governing thrift capital reserves were both foreseeable and likely when these parties contracted with the Government, as even the Government agrees. It says in its brief to this Court that "in light of the frequency with which federal capital requirements had changed in the past ..., it would have been unreasonable for Glendale, FSLIC, or the Bank Board to expect or rely upon the fact that those requirements would remain unchanged"....

   2

      . . .

   As to each of the contracts before us, our agreement with the conclusions of the Court of Federal Claims and the Federal Circuit forecloses any defense of legal impossibility, for those courts found that the Bank Board resolutions, Forbearance Letters, and other documents setting forth the accounting treatment to be accorded supervisory goodwill generated by the transactions were not mere statements of then-current regulatory policy, but in each instance were terms in an allocation of risk of regulatory change that was essential to the contract between the parties. Given that the parties went to considerable lengths in procuring necessary documents and drafting broad integration clauses to incorporate their terms into the contract itself, the Government's suggestion that the parties meant to say only that the regulatory treatment laid out in these documents would apply as an initial matter, subject to later change at the Government's election, is unconvincing. It would, indeed, have been madness for respondents to have engaged in these transactions with no more protection than the Government's reading would have given them, for the very existence of their institutions would then have been in jeopardy from the moment their agreements were signed.

*   *   *

   We affirm the Federal Circuit's ruling that the United States is liable to respondents for breach of contract. Because the Court of Federal Claims has not yet determined the appropriate measure or amount of damages in this case, we remand for further proceedings.

   It is so ordered.

Concurrence: Justice BREYER, concurring.

   I join the plurality opinion because, in my view, that opinion is basically consistent with the following understanding of what the dissent and the Government call the "unmistakability doctrine." The doctrine appears in the language of earlier cases, where the Court states that "sovereign power, even when unexercised, is an enduring presence that governs all contracts subject to the sovereign's jurisdiction, and will remain intact unless surrendered in unmistakable terms." The Government and the dissent believe that this language normally shields the Government from contract liability where a change in the law prevents it from carrying out its side of the bargain. In my view, however, this language, while perhaps appropriate in the circumstances of the cases in which it appears, was not intended to displace the rules of contract interpretation applicable to the Government as well as private contractors in numerous ordinary cases, and in certain unusual cases, such as this one....

      . . .

Concurrence: Justice SCALIA, concurring in the judgment.

I agree with the plurality that the contracts at issue in this case gave rise to an obligation on the part of the Government to afford respondents favorable accounting treatment, and that the contracts were broken by the Government's discontinuation of that favorable treatment, as required by FIRREA, 12 U.S.C. § 1464(t). My reasons for rejecting the Government's defenses to this contract action are, however, quite different from the plurality's, so I must write separately to state briefly the basis for my vote.

The plurality dispenses with three of the four "sovereign" defenses raised by the Government simply by characterizing the contracts at issue as "risk-shifting agreements" that amount to nothing more than "promises by the Government to insure [respondents] against any losses arising from future regulatory change." Thus understood, the plurality explains, the contracts purport, not to constrain the exercise of sovereign power, but only to make the exercise of that power an event resulting in liability for the Government—with the consequence that the peculiarly sovereign defenses raised by the Government are simply inapplicable. This approach has several difficulties, the first being that it has no basis in our cases, which have not made the availability of these sovereign defenses (as opposed to their validity on the merits) depend upon the nature of the contract at issue. But in any event, it is questionable whether, even as a matter of normal contract law, the exercise in contract characterization in which the plurality engages is really valid. . . .

. . .

Like THE CHIEF JUSTICE, I believe that the unmistakability doctrine applies here, but unlike him I do not think it forecloses respondents' claims. In my view, the doctrine has little if any independent legal force beyond what would be dictated by normal principles of contract interpretation. . . .

. . .

Finally, in my view the Government cannot escape its obligations by appeal to the so-called "sovereign acts" doctrine. . . . In my view the "sovereign acts" doctrine adds little, if anything at all, to the "unmistakability" doctrine, and is avoided whenever that one would be—i.e., whenever it is clear from the contract in question that the Governmentwas committing itself not to rely upon its sovereign acts in asserting (or defending against) the doctrine of impossibility, which is another way of saying that the Government had assumed the risk of a change in its laws. . . .

For the foregoing reasons, I concur in the judgment.

Dissent: Chief Justice REHNQUIST, dissenting.

The plurality's opinion works sweeping changes in two related areas of the law dealing with Government contracts. It drastically reduces the scope of the unmistakability doctrine, shrouding the residue with clouds of uncertainty, and it limits the sovereign acts doctrine so that it will have virtually no future application. I respectfully dissent.

I

The plurality properly recognizes that the unmistakability doctrine is a "special rule" of Government contracting which provides, in essence, a "canon of contract construction that surrenders of sovereign authority must appear in unmistakable terms." Exercises of the sovereign authority include of course the power to tax and, relevant to this case, the authority to regulate.

. . .

These cases have stood until now for the well-understood proposition . . . a waiver of sovereign authority will not be implied, but instead must be surrendered in unmistakable terms. Today, however, the plurality drastically limits the circumstances under which the doctrine will apply by drawing a distinction never before seen in our caselaw. . . .

. . .

II

The plurality also makes major changes in the existing sovereign acts doctrine which render the doctrine a shell. The plurality formally acknowledges the classic statement of the doctrine in *Horowitz v. United States* quoting: "'[i]t has long been held by the Court of Claims that the United States when sued as a contractor cannot be held liable for an obstruction of the performance of the particular contract resulting from its public and general acts as a sovereign.'" The plurality says that this statement cannot be taken at face value, however, because it reads "the essential point" of *Horowitz* to be "to put the Government in the same position that it would have enjoyed as a private contractor." But neither *Horowitz*, nor the Court of Claims cases upon which it relies, confine themselves to so narrow a rule. . . .

. . .

III

. . .

IV

. . .

V

A moment's reflection suggests that the unmistakability doctrine and the sovereign acts doctrine are not entirely separate principles. To the extent that the unmistakability doctrine is faithfully applied, the cases will be rare in which close and debatable situations under the sovereign acts doctrine are presented. I do not believe that respondents met either of these tests, and I would reverse the judgment of the Court of Appeals for the Federal Circuit outright or remand to that court for reconsideration in light of these tests as I have enunciated them.